THE KEEPER OF THE LIGHT.

EXPOSED STAIRWAY,
POINT REYES LIGHTHOUSE.

COVER:

"Built on an elevation three hundred feet above the sea, this beacon is reached by an exposed stairway of seven hundred and fifty steps. When storms are at their worst spray dashes up two hundred feet, falling upon the building that shelters the duplex 'siren' or fog whistle. The 'siren' of Point Reyes is heard twelve miles off the coast, and sings her mournful song eighty-three and one-third days in the year, the months of July and August being generally the most steeped in fog. The light, which owes its power to one thousand and thirty separate pieces of wonderfully adjusted glass, revolves every two minutes and flashes from the bull's eye at intervals of five seconds."

THE MONTAUK LIGHT.

Copyright ©1993
Vistabooks Publishing
Box 29D/Blue River Rt.
Silverthorne, CO 80498

ISBN 0-89646-086-X

Library of Congress Cataloging-in-Publication Data
Nordhoff, Charles, 1830-1901.
   The lighthouses of the United States in 1874 / by Charles Nordhoff
with Life in a Lighthouse, Life on the South Shoals lightship, and
Heroism in the lighthouse service / by Gustav Kobbe.
      p.   cm.
   "Nordhoff's material first appeared in 1874 in Harper's magazine
... Kobbe's articles appeared in Century magazine ... in 1891, 1894,
and 1897."
   ISBN 0-89646-086-X : $5.95
   1. Lighthouses of the United States--History.   I. Kobbé,Gustav,
1857-1918. Selections. 1992. II. Title.
VK1023.N67 1992
387.1'55--dc20   92-18576
                                                       CIP

THE LIGHT-HOUSES OF THE UNITED STATES IN 1874

by Charles Nordhoff

with

LIFE IN A LIGHTHOUSE,
LIFE ON THE SOUTH SHOALS LIGHTSHIP, and
HEROISM IN THE LIGHTHOUSE SERVICE

by Gustav Kobbe

EDITOR'S PREFACE

Here we reprint four articles on that romantic historic aspect of the maritime industry — the lighthouse. The first is a history and survey of lighthouses to 1874; the second gives insights into the keepers' lives in one of the most exposed lighthouses ever built — Minot's Ledge outside Boston Harbor; the third portrays the role played by off-coast lightships as seen by the sailors who manned one off Nantucket Island; and the fourth gives incidents of devotion to the lighthouse service and to mankind far beyond the call of duty. Together, these writings are assured continuing popularity with readers, as now lighthouses are not only still intriguing for their function and architecture but many are historic structures that recall exciting dramas of the past. Several are in areas operated by the National Park Service and are open to the public or are used in presenting the stories of the sea to visitors.

BARNEGAT LIGHT-HOUSE.

The 1874-1894 period when these articles appeared was near the heyday for the lighthouse. The United States already had an extensive system of lighting shoreline hazards along the shipping lanes. This was necessary because shipping had been growing as an American industry for years. If there is any further need to show the importance of lighthouses at this time, it can be pointed out that many were the objects of control by the opposing forces during the Civil War. Later, the need for lights on the shoals and shores was to decline with the advent of electronic navigational aids. Yet many of the most exposed points are still protected by lights, constantly manned.

Author Nordhoff reflects the technological enthusiasm of his time, giving us many details and facts of his period. He even tells us how to build a lighthouse! Similarly, Kobbe's articles present observations from his first-hand experience, involving more than casual visits to the Minot's Ledge Lighthouse and the South Shoals Lightship including plenty of interaction with the "inmates".

Nordhoff's material first appeared in 1874 in *Harper's Magazine,* a national periodical of that time for which he contributed other articles on California, Hawaii, and Mount Desert (in Maine). He also had published books to his credit. Kobbe's articles appeared in *Century Magazine,* also a national journal, in 1891, 1894, and 1897. Most of the illustrations accompanied the original articles; others have been added from contemporary sources, such as *Picturesque America* (1872), *Harper's Magazine* (1869, 1874, 1875, 1878), *Scribner's Monthly* (1873), *The Memorial Story of America* (1892), *America Illustrated* (1883), and *Picturesque California* (1888).

Withal, this concise book gives a good insight into an early phase of an important American industry, and, through it, into early America itself.

William R. Jones
Series Editor

A LIGHT-SHIP.

THE LIGHT-HOUSES OF THE UNITED STATES.

By CHARLES NORDHOFF.

FIRE ISLAND LIGHT, NEW YORK.

THE first act of Congress relating to light-houses was passed August 7, 1789. It provided that "all expenses which shall accrue from and after the 15th day of August, 1789, in the necessary support, maintenance, and repairs of all light-houses, beacons, buoys, and public piers, erected, placed, or sunk before the passing of this act, at the entrance of or within any bay, inlet, harbor, or port of the United States, for rendering the navigation thereof easy and safe, shall be defrayed out of the Treasury of the United States."

Seven months later, March 26, 1790, the same words were re-enacted, but with a proviso that "none of the said expenses shall continue to be so defrayed by the United States after the expiration of one year from the day aforesaid, unless such light-houses, beacons, buoys, and public piers shall in the mean time be ceded to and vested in the United States by the State or States respectively in which the same lie, together with the lands and tenements thereunto belonging, and *together with the jurisdiction of the same.*"

Before this the States which possessed sea-ports had controlled and supported each its own light-houses; by these two acts Congress prepared to assume the control of these aids to navigation and commerce, as the Constitution required; and ever since the Federal government has not only maintained and supported the light-houses, but it has also owned them, and a sufficient space of ground about them for all necessary ends. And thus it was that in the first proclamation of Mr. Lincoln, in 1861, he announced his purpose to recover and maintain possession of all forts, *light-houses,* etc.

The Federal government has not in any case erected a light-house until the State government had first ceded both the land on which it was to stand and the jurisdiction over it.

BERGEN POINT LIGHT-HOUSE, NEW JERSEY.

In March, 1815, twenty-six years after the first act quoted above, the government maintained eighty-four light-houses. In September, 1872, it maintained 573 light-houses and twenty-two light-ships, besides thirty-three fog-signals worked by steam or hot-air engines, 354 beacons, and 2762 buoys. There are now 809 light-keepers.

In 1815 light-houses were placed on the coasts of only eleven States; and Massachusetts had twenty lights, New York and Connecticut five each, Virginia and North Carolina four, and so on.

The first light-house was ceded to the Federal government by the State of Virginia, November 13, 1789. The cession included "two acres in the county of Princess Ann, the headland of Cape Henry," with a "reservation of fishing rights, and the hauling of seines." The next act of cession was in May, 1790, by Connecticut, of the "light-house at New London, and certain rocks and ledges off against the harbor of New London, called Race Rock, Black Ledge, and Goshen Reef, together with the buoys."

In June of the same year Massachusetts made a wholesale cession of eight pieces of real estate, with the light-houses on them or to be put on them; in November, 1790, New Jersey gave to the Federal government " a lot of about four acres at the point of Sandy Hook," in Monmouth County; and in 1792 New York ceded "Montauk Point, called Turtle Hill, in Suffolk County."

The history of our light-houses is really contained to a large extent in the laws of Congress relating to them. Thus in 1819 Congress appropriated $3027, in addition to other sums previously given, to make up the salaries of light-keepers to $350 per annum. In 1822 $8240 were appropriated to buy a patent light of David Melville, and place it in the light-houses. In 1825 it was enacted that " if any person or persons shall hold out or show any false light or lights, or extinguish any true light, with the

THATCHER'S ISLAND (CAPE ANN, MASSACHUSETTS), LIGHT AND FOG SIGNALS.

intention to bring any ship or vessel, boat or raft, being or sailing upon the sea, into danger or distress or shipwreck, every such person so offending, his or her counselors, aiders, and abettors, shall be deemed guilty of felony, and shall, on conviction thereof, be punished by a fine not exceeding four thousand dollars, and imprisonment and confinement to hard labor not exceeding ten years, according to the aggravation of the offense."

It is said that evil-minded persons on the Bahamas and elsewhere used systematically to hang out false lights to lure ships off their course and on to reefs, and that their rude method for imitating a revolving or flash light was to tie a lantern to a horse's tail and walk the animal around in a circle.

Until 1852 the light-houses were under the superintendence of the Fifth Auditor of the Treasury, who had other matters to attend to, was not himself chosen as an expert in light-house construction or maintenance, and had no authority to employ skilled assistants. There had been such constant and urgent complaints of the deficiencies of our

light-house system that a commission of proper persons was at last sent to Europe to inquire into the management of light-houses there, and in consequence of their report the present Light-house Board was constituted by act of Congress in August, 1852. This act authorized and required the President to appoint immediately two officers of the navy of high rank, one officer of the Engineer Corps, one of the Topographical Engineers, and two civilians of high scientific attainments; also an officer of the navy and one of the engineers to be secretaries. These together were constituted the Light-house Board, and to it was given charge of the erection, repair, and maintenance of all light-houses, light-ships, beacons, and buoys, with full powers. The Secretary of the Treasury was made ex officio president of the board.

The labors of this Light-house Board have placed our light service, which was once the worst in the world, at the head of all for the excellence of its different devices for relieving navigation of risks, and making our harbors easily accessible. All the most ap-

LIGHT-HOUSE AT TRIMBLE SHOALS, VIRGINIA.

proved modern improvements in lenses, reflectors, and lamps have been introduced; the many difficulties in building light-houses which are found on our long and varied coastline have been overcome with engineering skill and ingenuity highly creditable to our officers; and Congress, dealing liberally with this branch of the service, has enabled the board to perfect their work in all respects.

The Light-house Board is at present composed of the Secretary of the Treasury as ex officio President; Professor Joseph Henry, LL.D., Secretary of the Smithsonian Institution, Chairman; Brevet Major-General A. A. Humphreys, Chief of Engineers, U.S.A.; Brevet Major-General J. G. Barnard, Colonel of Engineers, U.S.A.; Professor Benjamin Peirce, LL.D., Superintendent of the United States Coast Survey; Captain John Lee Davis, U.S.N.; and Commodore Foxhall A. Parker, U.S.N.; with Rear-Admiral C. S. Boggs as Naval Secretary, and Major George H. Elliot, of the Engineers, as Engineer Secretary. The two secretaries are members of the board, and vote as such in its deliberations. They and Professor Henry are the able and capable members of the board on duty in the office at Washington. Admiral Shubrick was the first chairman of the board.

Besides the Congressional enactments punishing the destruction or disturbance of light-houses and buoys, many of the States impose penalties, either fine or imprisonment, or both, for such offenses.

There are thirteen light-house districts, beginning in Maine, and ending on the Pacific coast, and competent officers are detailed in each district to superintend new structures and repairs, and to see that supplies are constantly sent as needed.

A light-house keeper is required by the government to be over eighteen years old, to be able to read and write, and to be competent for his duties. "Women and servants must not be employed in the management of the lights, except by the special authority of the department."

There are six orders of lights in our service, the first being established to give warning of the approach to land, and the others being subsidiary, to mark headlands and points in bays, rivers, and lakes. There are white and red lights; fixed, revolving, and flash lights; and the revolving lights have different intervals, from a minute and a half to ten seconds. There are also fixed white lights showing a red flash at intervals; and in some cases two and even three fixed white lights mark a headland. Thus, on Cape Cod, Chatham has two lights, and Nausett three in a row. These differences are made to enable mariners the more readily and surely to distinguish lights apart, and thus to be certain what point or headland they are approaching at night. For the same reasons light-ships are numbered, and have their numbers painted on their sides. Buoys, too, are set in regular order for the better guidance of seamen. Thus, on entering a bay or harbor, the ship leaves red buoys, with even numbers, on her starboard, and black buoys, with odd numbers, on her port side. Where a buoy marks an obstruction in mid-channel which may be passed on either side, it is painted with horizontal red and black stripes; but if the buoy is striped white and black perpendicularly, this denotes that you must pass close to it to avoid danger. Perches with balls and cages on buoys denote that they are placed at turning-points in the channel. Thus it will be seen that, by various ingenious expedients, as little as possible is left to chance or guess-work; and the seaman who has his chart before him, and understands these simple regulations, can find his way into any of our ports.

All lights on the St. Lawrence, and on all our Northern lakes and their bays, are discontinued on the 1st of January, and relit only when the ice melts and navigation reopens.

The building of a light-house often demands the utmost skill, ingenuity, and knowledge of the engineer; and the illustrations in this article show how varying is the problem presented. Some are built of stones fastened together with heavy iron clamps; some, entirely of iron, look like a gigantic spider squatting on the water. Some, placed on low beaches or rocks, need to be tall towers. Others, like Point Reyes, in California, perched on high bluffs and cliffs, are only big enough to contain the lantern and its apparatus. In many cases light-houses are built complete at some foundry, and then transported to their proper place. In others men must work amidst the surf under such difficulties that in laying the foundations of Minot's Ledge Light-house, on the Massachusetts coast, one of the famous achievements in this branch of engineering, General Alexander, the distinguished officer who superintended the construction, was able to get but thirty hours of work done in the first year, and one hundred and fifty-seven hours in the second year.

Nor do ingenuity and care cease when the light-house is built and the keeper installed. Most of our light-houses are on barren, desolate, and exposed points of the coast. In some of them the keepers can not communicate at all with the shore during the winter months, and in such cases supplies of all kinds for the lights and the keepers must be accumulated beforehand. In many fresh-

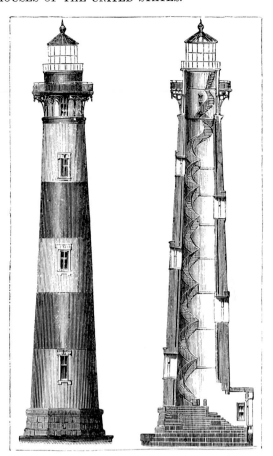

LIGHT-HOUSE, BODY'S ISLAND, NORTH CAROLINA.

water for the keeper and his family has to be caught in cisterns; and there is an official circular to light-keepers, telling them how to avoid the poisonous effect of the water dripping from the leads of the light-houses by putting powdered chalk into the cistern, and occasionally stirring it. In many places it has been found that cattle, attracted to the light at night, destroyed the strong-rooted grass which holds down sand dunes, and thus exposed the light-house itself to destruction; and in such cases a considerable area of land must be fenced in to exclude these beasts. On stormy nights sea-fowl are apt to dash themselves against the lantern glasses, blinded probably by the glare of the lights, and all light-keepers are specially warned in their printed instructions to be on the watch for such an accident, and extra panes of glass, fixed in frames, are always in readiness in every light-house, to substitute for those which may thus be broken.

In fact, the Light-house Board carries on and provides for an infinite number of details, many of them petty, but none unimportant. It must provide oil for the lamps, and oil butts must be ingeniously contrived so as to exclude air from their contents. It must keep a store of wicks, and of lamp scissors to trim the wicks; it must provide the most durable and economical paint for the iron of the lanterns; it has to send on supplies of food; and for the more complicated lights of the higher orders it has not only to provide expensive machinery, but must also keep on hand delicate yet simple tests by the help of which the light-keeper may be able daily to see that his lamp is set in the exact plane, and that his wicks are trimmed precisely high enough. It must provide such seemingly trifling articles as dusting and feather brushes, linen aprons, rouge powder, prepared whiting, spirits of wine, buff or chamois skins, and linen cleaning cloths, and, what will appeal to the sensibilities of most country housekeepers, the Light-house Board must keep on hand at each light-house a sufficient supply of glass chimneys for the lamps. No doubt the board possesses the invaluable secret of making chimneys last a long time, and no doubt many an excellent housekeeper who reads this would like to ask Professor Henry what kind of lamp chimneys he has found to be the most lasting and the least liable to crack.

There is a printed book of one hundred and fifty-two pages specially devoted to "instructions and directions to light-keepers," and in this they receive explicit commands not only for their daily duties, but for all possible or imaginable accidents and emergencies. The first article of these instructions announces the fundamental duty of the light-keeper: "The light-house and light-vessel lamps shall be lighted, and the lights exhibited for the benefit of mariners, *punctually at sunset daily.* Light-house and light-vessel lights are to be kept burning brightly, free from smoke, and at their greatest attainable heights, *during each entire night*, from sunset to sunrise;" and it is added that "the height of the flame must be frequently measured during each watch at night, by the scale graduated by inches and tenths of an inch, with which keepers are provided." Finally, "All light-house and light-vessel lights shall be extinguished punctually at sunrise, and every thing put in order for lighting in the evening by ten o'clock A.M. daily."

It would be tedious, and take more space than we have to spare, to give even a bald list of all the tools and materials required in a first-class light-house. A glance over the index of the volume of directions shows that it contains instructions for cleaning, placing, removing, and preserving the lamp chimneys; for cleaning the lamps; for keeping the lantern free from ice and snow; for preserving the whiting, rouge powder, etc.; for using two or three dozen tools; for preserving and economically using the oil, filling the lamp, using the damper; for precautions against fire; "how to trim the wicks;" and for dozens of other details of the light-keeper's daily duties.

LIGHT-HOUSE, CLEVELAND, OHIO—LAKE ERIE.

The keeper is required to enter in a journal (daily) all events of importance occurring in and near his tower, and also to keep a table of the expenditure of oil and other stores. Besides the officer who is district light-house inspector, and who may make his examinations at any time, there are experts called "lampists," who pass from light to light, making needed repairs, and also taking care that the machinery of the light is in order, and that it is properly attended to by the keeper.

In the construction of light-houses many nice points have to be borne in mind. For instance, on the Atlantic coast it is found difficult very often to raise the towers high enough so as to let the lights be seen at a great distance. But on our Pacific coast the difficulty is often to get them low enough. The coast of California is mostly mountainous and precipitous : the fog hangs low on the mountain-sides; and if lights were placed too high, they would be obscured by the fog. Our Pacific coast, by-the-way, is far more foggy than the Atlantic side; and fog-signals are of more importance between San Francisco and the mouth of the Columbia than along the whole shore-line from Calais to St. Augustine. The proper height for a sea-coast light is about one hundred and fifty feet above the sea-level; but on the California coast it is rarely that room can be got for a light-house so low down as this. The fine light at Point Reyes stands two hundred and ninety-six feet above the sea, and that of Point Loma, at the entrance of San Diego Bay, is nearly five hundred feet above the sea. Point Reyes light can be seen at a distance of twenty-four nautical miles when the weather is clear; when it is foggy, a steam fog-whistle warns the mariner to keep off a line of coast which is as dangerous to a ship as a shark's mouth would be to a man. The light-houses,

light-ships, buoys, beacons, fog-signals, machine-shops, and other property controlled by the Light-house Board, are worth between forty and fifty millions of dollars. The whole of this is a free gift of the American people to the world. Other nations exact light-house dues which to a great extent defray the expense of maintaining their lights, but our government has made all lights free to the mariners of all nations. The whole establishment is sustained by annual appropriations of Congress.

The present pay of light-house keepers varies according to the importance of the light and the responsibility put upon the keeper. The Congressional appropriation covers an average salary of six hundred dollars per annum. The keeper of Minot's Ledge, on the Massachusetts coast, receives $1000, while some keepers receive but $350.

The cost of light-houses varies as much as the salaries of the keepers. Some light-houses cost ten thousand dollars; Minot's Ledge light cost a quarter of a million; and the light-house on Spectacle Reef, on the coast of Lake Huron, cost $300,000. A pic-

LIGHT-HOUSE AT SPECTACLE REEF, LAKE HURON.

ture of the last-named light-house is given on page 11, and the following account of the difficulties encountered in preparing for its construction will give an idea of what natural obstacles have often to be overcome in this kind of building. The account is taken from the official report:

The site of the tower being determined, and the proper soundings and surveys made, a crib ninety-two feet square was built, having a central opening forty-eight feet square to receive the cofferdam which was to form the pier of protection, as well as the landing-place for materials. This huge crib was floated to its place.

In order to get accurate soundings to guide in shaping the bottom of the crib, and to fix with a degree of certainty the position of these soundings and that to be occupied by the crib, four temporary cribs, each fifteen feet by twenty-five feet, of round timber, were placed in from eight to ten feet of water, in a line corresponding with the proposed eastern face of the pier of protection, and filled to the level of the water with ballast stone. These four cribs were then decked over and connected together. Upon the pier thus formed about seventy cords of ballast stone were placed, ready at the proper time to be thrown into the crib forming the pier of protection.

The lower two complete courses of the pier of protection having been fastened together by screw-bolts, forming a raft, constituting a ground-plan of the pier of protection, were then towed to the reef, where framed to the reef, and moored directly over the position to be occupied by the finished pier. Its position was marked upon the temporary pier referred to above, and soundings taken at intervals of two feet along each timber in the raft, thus obtaining accurate contours of the surface of

POINT REYES LIGHT-HOUSE, PACIFIC COAST.

the reef within the limits of these timbers. The raft was then towed back to the harbor, hauled out upon ways, and by means of wedges of timber the bottom was made to conform to the surface of the reef. The raft, now become the bottom of the pier of protection, was then launched, and additional courses of timber built upon it, until its draught of water was just sufficient to permit its being floated into position on the reef, at which time it was estimated that the top of the pier would be one foot out of water.

The depth of water on the reef at the points to be occupied by the four corners of the pier of protection was found to be as follows: At northeast corner, ten feet six inches; at northwest corner, thirteen feet; at southwest corner, fourteen feet six inches; and at southeast corner, nine feet six inches—the position to be occupied by the pier of protection having been so chosen that the sides would correspond to the cardinal points of the compass. Meanwhile five barges at the harbor had been loaded with ballast stone, making, together with those on the temporary pier at the reef, 290 cords (about 1800 tons) at command, with which to load the pier of protection and secure it to the reef as soon as it should be placed in position.

On the evening of the 18th of July, 1871, every thing being in readiness, and the wind, which had been blowing freshly from the northwest for three days previously, having somewhat moderated, at 8 P.M. the tugs *Champion* (screw-propeller) and *Magnet* (side-wheel) took hold of the immense crib and started to tow it to the reef, fifteen miles distant, followed by the *Warrington* (screw-propeller), having in tow the schooner *Belle*, the two having on board a working force of 140 men, the tug *Stranger* (screw-propel-

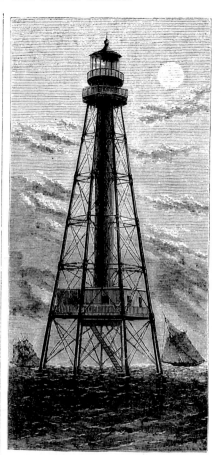

LIGHT-HOUSE AT ALLIGATOR REEF, FLORIDA.

ler), with barges *Ritchie* and *Emerald*, and the tug *Hand*, with two scows of the Light-house Establishment. The barge *Table Rock*, with fifty cords of stone on board, was left in reserve at the harbor. The construction scow, with tools, etc., on board, was towed with the crib. At 2 A.M. next morning, six hours after starting, the fleet hove to off the reef, awaiting daylight and the abatement of the wind, which had again freshened up. At 6½ A.M., it having moderated, the pier, with considerable difficulty, was placed in position, and after being secured to the temporary pier and the moorings previously set for the purpose, all hands went to work throwing the ballast stone into the compartments, and by 4 P.M. succeeded in getting into it about 200 cords, or 1200 tons. By this time the wind was blowing freshly, and the sea running so high as to make it necessary to stop work for the time, but early next morning all the reserve stone was put into the compartments.

After the pier was in position the schooner *Belle* was moored on the reef to serve as

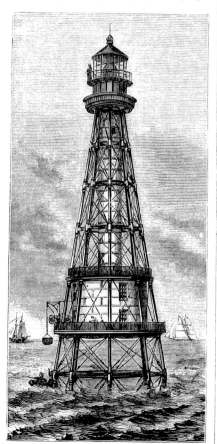

LIGHT-HOUSE AT TRINITY SHOAL, GULF OF MEXICO.

LIGHT-HOUSE AT PIEDRAS BLANCAS, CALIFORNIA.

quarters for the working force, which proceeded to build up the pier to the required height above water (twelve feet). On the 12th of September the pier had been built up to its full height, and by the 20th of September quarters for the workmen had been completed upon it, which were at once occupied, and the *Belle* returned to the harbor.

By means of a submarine diver the bed-rock within the opening of the pier was then cleared off, and the work of constructing the coffer-dam was taken in hand. The coffer-dam itself consisted of a hollow cylinder, forty-one feet in diameter, composed of wooden staves, each four inches by six, and fifteen feet long. The cylinder was braced and trussed internally, and hooped with iron externally, so as to give it the requisite strength. It was put together at the surface of the water, and when complete was lowered into position on the bed-rock by means of iron screws.

•As soon as it rested on the rock (which was quite irregular in contour), each stave was driven down so as to fit as closely as it would admit, and a diver filled all openings between its lower end and the rock with Portland cement. A loosely twisted rope of oakum was then pressed close down into the exterior angle between the coffer-dam and rock, and outside of this a larger rope made of hay. The pumping machinery having meanwhile been placed in readiness, the coffer-dam was pumped dry, and on the same day (14th October) a force of stone-cutters descended to the bottom and commenced the work of leveling off the bed-rock, and preparing it to receive the first course of masonry.

The bed-rock was found to consist of dolomitic limestone, confirming the previous examinations, highest on the western side, toward the deepest water, and sloping gradually toward the eastern. In order to make a level bed for the first course of masonry it was necessary to cut down about two feet on the highest side, involving a large amount of hard labor, rendered more difficult by the water forcing its way up through seams in the rock. But the work was finally accomplished, the bed being as carefully cut and leveled as any of the courses of masonry.

The first course of masonry was then set, completing it on the 27th of October. While setting this course much trouble was caused by the water, already referred to as forcing its way up through seams in the rock, which attacked the mortar-bed. For this reason water was let into the dam every evening, and pumped out next morning, to give the mortar time to harden during the night. This mortar was composed of equal parts of Portland cement and screened siliceous sand. Specimens of it obtained the following spring, after being in place under water for seven months, were quite as hard or harder than either the bed-rock or the stone used in building the tower.

The weather having now become very

boisterous, with frequent snow-squalls, often interrupting the work, and the setting of any additional stone requiring the removal of a portion of the most important of the interior braces of the coffer-dam, it was deemed prudent to close the work for the season. This, too, would give ample time for the hardening of the mortar used in bedding the stone, and the concrete used for filling cavities in the bed-rock, as well as the space between the outside of the first course and the coffer-dam, which was solidly filled with concrete to the top of the first course. Therefore the coffer-dam was allowed to fill with water, the process being hastened by boring holes through it to admit the water, and it was secured to prevent its being lifted by the ice during the winter.

The machinery was laid up, and on the last of October all the working force, except two men, was removed. These two men were left to attend to the fourth-order light which had been established on the top of the men's quarters, and the fog-signal, consisting of a whistle attached to one of the steam-boilers. At the close of navigation they were taken off the pier by the light-house tender *Haze*.

The degree of success of this novel coffer-dam may be inferred from the fact that although prepared with pumps of an aggregate capacity of five thousand gallons per minute, not more than a capacity of seven hundred gallons was used, except when emptying the coffer-dam, and then only to expedite the work. Once emptied, a small proportion of this capacity was ample to keep the coffer-dam free from water; and this at a depth of twelve feet of water, on rock, at a distance of nearly eleven miles from the nearest land. Every person connected with the work may well feel a just pride in its success. All the stone which had been delivered at the harbor, consisting of the first five courses (each course two feet

thick), having been cut by this time, the work there was also closed.

The season opened a month later in 1872 than in 1871, consequently work was not resumed at the harbor until the 3d of May, and upon the reef until the 20th of the same month. On the 13th of May the ice in the coffer-dam was still a compact mass, of some feet in thickness. Masses of ice still lay on top of the pier itself. As soon as any thing could be done, the ice still remaining was cleared out of the coffer-dam, the machinery put in order, the braces removed from the interior of the coffer-dam, and then the work of setting additional courses began.

The work upon the tower was carried on at such a rate that one entire course of masonry was set, drilled, and bolted complete every three days.

The Spectacle Reef tower was founded upon a rock the highest part of which was ten feet under water. The rock on which the Minot's Ledge light-tower stands had its highest part on a level with the water at extreme low tide and in very smooth weather. The work on Minot's Ledge, how-

LIGHT-HOUSE AT CALCASIEU, GULF COAST OF LOUISIANA.

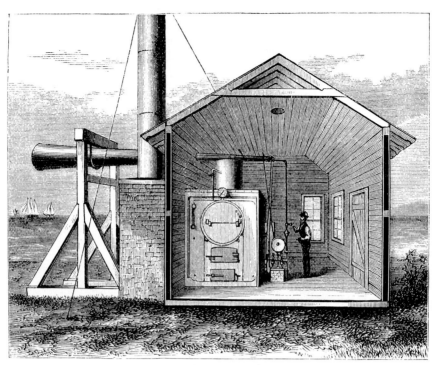

OPERATION OF A SIREN (STEAM FOG-HORN)—SECTIONAL VIEW.

ever, was more difficult, because of the ocean swell which there rolls in.

The lenses used to enforce, concentrate, and direct the higher grades of lights cost various prices, up to eleven or twelve thousand dollars. The lamp of a first-order sea-coast light-house has four concentric wicks, the outer one being four inches in diameter. The oil is pumped up by clock-work or other machinery so as to feed these wicks constantly to their utmost, that they may give out as much light as possible. The Fresnel lens now comes in to save all the rays of light which have thus carefully been created, and to concentrate them and send them forth in that direction only in which they are required. Briefly described, the invention of Fresnel consists in surrounding the lamp by a series of prismatic rings of glass, each different from the others in its angles, but all cut mathematically to such angles that the rays which go above the proper plane and those which fall below shall be bent by refraction and reflection so as to become parallel with the lateral rays. Thus all the rays are saved and sent out in one sheet over the ocean. The construction of lenses for light-houses was described in an article in *Harper's Magazine* for February, 1869, and we will not, therefore, repeat it here. It is necessary, however, to say that one of the most important duties of the keeper of a light is to see daily that the light and the

lens are upon the exact and proper level. A deviation of only a fraction of an inch might throw the beam of light toward the sky or down toward the base of the light-tower, and thus make it useless to the mariner.

Formerly the best sperm-oil was used in light-house lamps. Colza or rape-seed oil was next introduced in Europe, and is still used there, as it is an excellent oil. It is, however, difficult in this country to get a sufficient quantity of the best kind, and our Light-house Board now uses the best quality of lard-oil, made on purpose for the establishment. Kerosene and other mineral oils have been used in the British Provinces and in Europe to some extent, but there are certain obvious risks attending them which prevent their use with us.

There are at this time half a dozen electric lights in Europe, but their number is not increasing. They have proved extremely expensive in the maintenance, requiring the use of steam-engines for generating the electricity. It is said that this light, which is, no doubt, more powerful than any other in clear weather, does not penetrate fog so well as the oil light.

Experience has shown our Light-house Board that the best light-keepers are old sailors and soldiers, and it is its desire, we have been told, that the maimed of those who served in the war for the Union should, where they are physically and mentally competent, receive these places. It is to be hoped that civil service reform will make its way also into this department of the government service, for the petty though important place of light-keeper has too often been made a political prize, and thus the service, which requires permanence, has been injured. The politicians of the baser sort have not seldom defeated the best intentions and desires of the board, and ousted a good man to put in one "useful at the polls." A merchant might as reasonably change his book-keeper for political reasons as the government change its light-keepers for this cause. In England the light-keeper holds his office for life or good behavior. When he enters the service he is rigidly examined as to his duties, and must produce the best evidence of good character and sound health. He begins at a less important light, on a low salary, and is promoted for skill and attention to his duties. To this, it is hoped, we shall presently come.

Fog-signals, many of which are required at different points on the Atlantic and Pacific coasts, are of several kinds. Some are steam-whistles, the sound of which is made deeper or louder by being sent through a trumpet; but the most effective is probably the Siren. This ingenious machine consists of a long trumpet and a steam-boiler. The sound is produced by the rapid revolution past each other of two flat disks pierced with a great number of small holes; a jet of steam under high pressure is projected against the disks, which revolve past each other more than a thousand times a minute; as the rows of small holes in the two disks come opposite each other, the steam vehemently rushes through and makes the singular and piercing noise which a Siren gives out. One of these machines, of which a drawing is given on page 476, costs about $3500 complete, with its trumpet, boiler, etc.

Daboll's trumpet is worked by an Ericsson engine, and requires no water for steam.

Congress rightly has great confidence in the scientific skill and integrity of the Light-house Board. At the last session, besides the usual appropriation for the maintenance of the light-house system, it gave the money needed to build forty new light-houses ·and ten steam fog-signals. If we ever have a merchant marine of our own again, our seamen will find the stormy and rock-bound coasts of their country well lighted for them.

"NOT LIGHTED."

Light-House, Buffalo.

Main Light, at Erie.

DRAWN BY CARLTON T. CHAPMAN.

JUPITER INLET.

ENGRAVED BY J. HELWELL.

LIGHT-HOUSE OF THE SOUTH FARALLON.

MINOT'S LEDGE LIGHT-HOUSE, MASSACHUSETTS.

POINT PINOS LIGHT HOUSE.

LIFE IN A LIGHTHOUSE.

(MINOT'S LEDGE.)

by Gustav Kobbe

WITH PICTURES BY W. TABER.

AS the billows roll in from the Atlantic toward the rocky shores of Cohasset, on the south side of Boston Bay, their onward sweep is checked by a round, gray, ancient-looking tower that rises out of the sea. On a calm day the waves swash around its base, meeting on the lee side in a spout that quivers the air, a column of liquid porphyry, to fall back again and be lost in a hundred eddies among hidden rocks, like the Little Minot and East Shag, that lie between the tower and the shore. In a stiff breeze each billow, as it strikes, sends a shower of glittering spray half-way up the tower's height of a hundred and fourteen feet, and a long breaker sweeps shoreward, its gleaming crest, which seems about to pour like a cataract into the trough of the sea, held in suspense by the mighty onrush of the wave from which it overhangs. But right in its course lies the Little Minot; and lo! the bold front of the breaker, with the power of the Atlantic at its back, is broken to foam as it closes in upon the ledge. Its crest, so long proudly poised, pours into the hollow; there is a moment of hissing and seething; a thousand white tongues are licking the jagged outcropping of rock; they meet, pass over and under one another in their undulations, swish up and swash back again, separate into countless miniature whirlpools — and then there is nothing left of the great wave but a circle of froth.

savagely upon the tower, dashing tons of spray high into the air above it — the shattered remnants of the heaving mass that a moment before struck the granite courses. For the sea meets its match in the lighthouse on Minot's Ledge. Yet the shattered wave has not spent

IN A NORTHEASTER.

ENGRAVED BY F. H. WELLINGTON.

But it is in a northeasterly storm that the old gray tower most grandly maintains its battle with the sea; for then the billows have had the broad expanse of storm-swept ocean over which to gather force. Long livid lines of breakers rush out from behind the threatful storm-clouds that lower upon the horizon, like the battalions of an army marshaled by the powers of the air and the sea against the structure that man has reared in defiance of their prerogative. Each wave hurls itself its fury all in vain. It, too, can boast its moment of triumph, for it has struck terror into some hearts — not into those of the lighthouse-keepers, for throughout the shock and confusion of the storm the vigil in the watch-room is faithfully maintained; but in the keepers' dwellings on shore, between which and Minot's Ledge gleam three miles of white water, — the winding-sheet of ships, — anxious faces at the windows are watching through the night for reassuring glimpses of the light,

which come only too fitfully when the tower is all "buried up" by the sea.

Landing on Minot's Ledge is easy enough in the summer time when the sea is smooth; but in winter there is hardly a time when the ladder that runs from the foot of the tower to the door forty feet above is of any service. Owing to the peculiar wash of the waves around the base, it is only on very rare occasions that a boat can lie near the ladder without danger of being swamped or dashed to pieces. In summer, when it is too rough to land by the ladder, visitors are hoisted up in a chair; but space in the tower being very contracted, the keepers limit the furnishings to the very minimum, and in the fall the chair is shipped to Cohasset, where it hibernates. When, last February, I landed at Minot's, or rather was hoisted into it, the steps could not be used. We had been in sight of the tower since we had put out from Boston Harbor; had seen it rising gray and grim in all its loneliness out of the waves. As the lighthouse tender *Geranium,* a low, broad, black side-wheel craft—not unlike a beetle in deliberateness of motion and looks, but nevertheless rejoicing in the title U. S. L. H. S.—headed for Minot's, and it had become apparent to the keepers that she was creeping toward the tower, a figure appeared at the door, and, climbing half-way down the ladder, hung to a rung with one hand, and, with an ax in the other, began chopping at something white which rose from the sea to where he stood. He looked like a pygmy hanging there against the forty feet of granite up which the ladder ran. Soon afterward he ascended the ladder slowly, as if almost exhausted, and another man descended and took his place. "The ladder is heavily iced up, and they 're trying to clear it," said the captain of the *Geranium,* who had trained a spy-glass on the tower.

Meanwhile the tender had been hove to and the boat lowered. Pulling to a spar-buoy some three hundred feet from the tower, we passed a line around it, and, paying out from the buoy, allowed the boat to drift within hailing distance of the keeper. The tower was weather-streaked, and its base up to high-water mark was covered with a greenish black ooze. Around the base the sea was gurgling. Occasionally a breaker swept threateningly toward the boat, and the mate in the stern would haul her in by the cable toward the buoy, while the crew

ENGRAVED BY CHARLES STATE.

A WINTER LANDING.

backed water clear of the combing crest, which would have swamped her but for this manœuvering. Out of the ocean before us rose course after course of solid masonry to a deep, narrow doorway far above us, where, his hands grasping iron supports, he himself leaning out over the water, stood what seemed from our distance a diminutive human figure in dark blue. The answer to our hail came back faintly above the noisy sea. It was too rough to land at the ladder, and even if it were not, the lower half was so thickly incrusted with ice that no one could retain a foothold on it; but if the block and tackle could be rigged before the sea roughened, I might be hoisted into the tower. The assistant inspector had told me before I left the tender that this might be the only way of landing me, adding, "If you don't like the looks of the rig, come back, and we'll try some other day"; so that I had determined to make the attempt, no matter at what risk. In a deep porthole two stories above the door a spar had been rigged. To this was attached a block through which ran a rope ending in a loop. A coil of line fastened to the loop was held in the hand of the keeper, who stood in the doorway. The boat was paid out from the buoy, the keeper threw the line, and as it fell across the boat one of the crew seized it and hauled it in. Straddling the loop, and grasping the rope above it with both hands, I gave the signal, and the keepers began hoisting, while one of the boat's crew slowly paid out the line to which the loop was attached. I was literally hanging between sea and sky, being hoisted upward and at the same time across toward the tower. It was a gray day. Where the sea below me shallowed over the jagged rocks around the base of the tower, I saw a tangle of slimy seaweed swirl half-way up to the surface and sink slowly out of sight. The little craft was now rising upon the waves, now lying in the trough of the sea, now backing toward the buoy, now moving away from it, according to the changing condition of the sea—and at Minot's it is ever changing. An accident to the boat or to the man who held the line attached to the loop, and no earthly power could have prevented my being dashed against the tower. But at last I had been raised to a level with the door, and was allowed to swing slowly into the arms of the keeper, who hauled me in, and was apparently as glad as I was to see me safely landed.

I found myself in a circular, brick-lined room, or rather cell, which received its only light through the deep, narrow door so high above the base of the tower that, as one looked out through it from the center of the room, it framed in nothing but a distant vista of heaving sea and gray, scurrying clouds. In the wall opposite

A SUMMER LANDING.

the door was a small, deep window, like the port-hole in a casemate. Its heavy wooden shutter was securely bolted, yet water was dripping from the granite recess into a bucket on the floor, with such force does the sea strike the tower on Minot's Ledge. An iron stairway curved along the wall through an iron ceiling to the story above. The granite floor was wet from spray that had been blown in through the doorway, and the roar of the sea reverberated within the confines of the room.

By all who are familiar with the dangers to which it is exposed and the difficulties which had to be overcome in its construction, the Minot's Ledge Lighthouse is considered a great work of engineering—greater, many experts think, than the famous Eddystone, because outlying ledges somewhat protect the latter against the assaults of the sea, and the rock on which

ENGRAVED BY R. C. COLLINS.

THE WRECK OF THE FIRST LIGHTHOUSE.

it stands, being all above water, offers a better foundation surface than Minot's. The Outer Minot, the most exposed rock among the ledges on which the Minot's Ledge Lighthouse stands, is entirely submerged at high tide. Not until three quarters ebb do the first jagged points jut out above the water, and preliminary surveys showed that a surface only thirty feet in diameter was exposed at extreme low tide.

The lighthouse on Minot's Ledge stands within the shadow of a tragedy. It is the second structure erected upon the ledge. The first lighthouse and the lives it held were claimed by the sea. Begun in 1847 and completed in November, 1848, it was overwhelmed in April, 1851. Its destruction was the most tragic event in the history of our lighthouse establishment. The structure was an octagonal tower supported upon wrought-iron piles strengthened by braces. The piles penetrated five feet into the rock. On the braces, thirty-four and a half feet above the rock, the keeper had constructed a platform for the storage of bulky articles, and had fastened to the lantern-deck, sixty-three feet above the rock, a five-and-a-half-inch hawser which he had anchored to a seven-ton granite block. Along this hawser articles were hoisted up to the platform, and there landed. These "improvements" were convenient—and fatal; not, however, to the keeper who made them, for he was on shore when the storm which has become historic for its fury burst over the coast.

On Monday, April 14, 1851, there was a strong easterly gale blowing. At that time there were on the tower two assistant keepers and a friend of the principal keeper. The visitor became frightened at the first indication of a storm, and, in response to a signal from the tower, a boat put off from Cohasset and took him ashore. On Tuesday the wind swung around to the northeast, the most dangerous quarter from which the elements can hurl themselves upon Minot's, as they then rejoice in the accumulated fury of miles of wind-torn sea. By the 16th it had increased to a hurricane, and the tower was so completely buried in the heavy seas that nothing of it could be seen by the group of anxious watchers at Cohasset. About four o'clock in the evening of the 16th the platform was washed ashore. Then the watchers knew that the water had risen to within seven feet of the tower. At nightfall it was seen that the light was burning. It was observed at fitful intervals until ten o'clock that night, when it was finally lost to sight. At one o'clock on the morning of Thursday, April 17, just at the turn of the flood, when the outstreaming tide and the inrushing hurricane met at Minot's, a violent tolling of the lighthouse bell was heard. After that no sound rose above the din of the storm. About six o'clock in the morning a man walking along the shore saw a chair washed up a little distance ahead of him. Examining it, he recognized it as having been in the watch-room of the tower. After this discovery no one had any doubts of the tragedy which had been enacted behind the curtain of the storm. When it lifted, naught was seen over Minot's Ledge but the sea, its white crests streaming triumphantly in the gale.

It is believed by those competent to judge of such matters that the destruction of the tower was due to the surface which the platform constructed by the keeper offered to the waves, and to the strain of the hawser upon the structure. Every time this hawser was struck by a sea it actually tugged at the tower. There seems also little doubt that the sum appropriated by Congress for the building of the lighthouse was insufficient by about two thirds for such a structure as the perilous situation called for.

When the site was visited after the disaster, the bent and broken stumps of the iron piling were found in the rocks. Their appearance indicated that before the tower fell it had been bent to leeward until it actually hung over the wild and crested waters. This brought to mind the sudden violent tolling of the bell at one o'clock in the morning of that fatal 17th of April. No other conclusion seems possible than that when the tower heeled over to leeward each wave, as it swept over the parapet, struck the bell and set it swinging, so that the sea itself tolled the knell of the souls it was doomed to claim.

There is an incident in the tragedy of Minot's Ledge that should always be remembered. Up to the last moment the men on the tower kept the light, for its gleam was seen through the storm-scud until the hurricane closed in too thick for the light to be visible. Of the men who thus did their duty face to face with death for the honor of the lighthouse service of the United States, one was a German, the other a Portuguese. No monument has been erected to these brave fellows; probably the idea of one has never been broached. Not even their names are remembered; for if you attempt to discover something of these humble heroes in Cohasset, all you will learn is that one was a "Dutchman" and the other a "Portugee."

"They hung to duty to the last," said the present keeper of Minot's Ledge Lighthouse, concluding his story of the tragedy to me one night in the watch-room, while a northeaster roared around the lantern, and the spray came rattling down upon it, the old tower meantime shaking the water off like a dog that has had a wetting. Such nights our thoughts naturally reverted to the men who had perished at their posts on the very spot where the tower in which

we sat was built. The body of one of them was found among the seaweed around East Shag. The other was never recovered.

Of these two whose spirit is it that is believed to revisit Minot's Ledge? For there have been keepers of the present tower who have affirmed that one of those who perished with the old lighthouse haunts the spot. Strange noises have been heard in the oil-room—sudden rattling of cans and clinking of glass, as if some one were at work there. Stories are also current of the mysterious filling of the lamp and cleaning of the lens and lantern. In the old tower, when a watch was at an end, the keeper in the watch-room summoned the keeper below by rapping on the stovepipe which ran up from the lower room, and the other keeper would rap in reply to notify the watch that he had heard the signal and would be up immediately. In the present tower the watch is called and the answer given by electric bells. One night, as the midnight watch was drawing to a close, the keeper in the watch-room, who had been brooding over the destruction of the old tower, quite unconsciously leaned forward and rapped with his pipe. A few minutes later he was startled to hear an answering rap from below. Every moment he expected the other keeper to appear and relieve him. After waiting in vain, he pressed the button of the electric bell, and after the usual interval the bell in the watch-room rang the reply from below, and the steps of the relieving watch were heard on the iron stairs. He had not heard the rapping, and therefore had made no reply, his first intimation of the change of watch having been the ringing of the bell!

The Minots are off the southeastern chop of Boston Bay. Vessels standing in for Boston Harbor, and losing their bearings in a northeaster, would be apt to be driven on the ledges, unless warned off by a friendly beacon. Indeed, here was, before the establishment of the light, a veritable ocean graveyard. Even since then there have been heartrending disasters, such as the breaking to pieces of the ship *St. John* on the Hogshead, when all but one of the hundred and sixty people aboard her were lost, the survivor being a woman who, lashed to a spar, was washed ashore in a half-frozen condition. Many corpses, among them women with children clasped to their breasts, drifted in on the "porridge-ice" with which the harbor was filled.

After the destruction of the first lighthouse, Congress made an appropriation for the building of another. The tower which now stands upon Minot's Ledge was designed by General J. G. Totten, and erected by Captain Barton S. Alexander, both of the Engineer Corps of the United States army. Captain Alexander's work on the tower is considered second in importance only to that of the designer; for, owing to the exposed site, many difficulties had to be overcome in the course of construction. Work could be carried on only from April to September, the sea being too rough at other times to admit of the workmen gaining a footing on the ledge, or even of approaching it with safety. The first blow was struck Sunday morning, July 1, 1855. The building of Minot's Ledge Lighthouse was a work for humanity, and therefore Sunday, the first day the weather had been propitious for beginning operations, was utilized. The weather allowed of only one hundred and thirty working hours at the ledge that entire season. Preparing partly submerged rock to receive the foundations of a granite tower is quite a different matter from digging a hole in the ground on shore. Guards in boats constantly plied round the ledge to pick up workmen who might be washed off into the sea, and their services were frequently required. Not until July 9, 1857, could the first stone be laid. During that season there were again only one hundred and thirty working hours at the ledge. Anticipating such a contingency, Captain Alexander had picked out a force of good all-round workmen, so that when work had to be suspended on the ledge the morale of his force would be maintained by keeping the men occupied on shore in shaping the granite blocks for the tower, and fitting the courses on a model, so that no time would be lost in correcting errors after the blocks had been shipped to the ledge. As a matter of fact, work on the model disclosed several miscalculations which would have caused annoying delay had they not been discovered in time to be rectified on shore. The tower was completed September 16, 1860, in 1102 hours and 21 minutes, at a cost of $300,000. In shape it is the frustum of a cone, one hundred and fourteen feet and one inch in height, including the lantern. The first full course of masonry is thirty feet in diameter. Except for a narrow well running down through the center to the rock, the tower is a piece of solid granite masonry to the store-room, forty feet above. The well, besides storing water for the keepers' use, serves as an indicator of danger; for should there be a crack in

the masonry, it would leak. The store-room is one of five stories above the solid base. Each consists of one circular room lined with brick, and has a deep port-hole. All the stairways in the tower are iron, and so are the ceilings, except that of the fifth story, which is granite, is arched, and forms the top of the tower proper. These rooms are fourteen feet in diameter. The watch-room, lantern, and

ENGRAVED BY H. DAVIDSON.
WATCHING THE LIGHT.

dome are built above the tower proper, the cornice of which forms a parapet around the watch-room, while part of the bronze metal ceiling of the latter serves the same purpose for the lantern-deck. The lantern is framed in iron, and iron supports slant from the edge of the lantern-parapet to the top of the framework.

The masonry work of the base is strengthened by eight iron shafts set in the rock at the same points as the piling of the first tower; there are dowels between each course in the base, and the courses above the base are dovetailed. Indeed, the whole tower is so closely bolted and knit together that it seems destined to last as long as the rock on which it stands.

Over the store-room is the kitchen, where the keepers also eat their meals. Above this is the bedroom of the assistant keepers, that of the keeper being on the third floor. Though furnished with only the most necessary articles, there is little moving room left. Toilet is made at the kitchen sink, an arrangement which experience has proved to be the simplest and the best adapted to the circumstances. The fourth floor is the oil-room, where the nights' supply of oil for the lamp is kept, the annual consumption being about 875 gallons. The watch-room—the drawing-room of Minot's Ledge Lighthouse—is above this. Here the keepers sit when they are not busy during the day, and from here they watch the light at night, the watches lasting from 4 P. M. to 8 P. M., 8 P. M. to 12 M., 12 M. to 4 A. M., 4 A. M. to 6 A. M.

The routine of duty on Minot's Ledge is the same as in any other lighthouse, but it is gone through under somewhat different circumstances. At the end of the dog-watch at 6 A. M., the assistant keeper, who also officiates as cook, prepares breakfast. This is usually ready by half-past six. The electric bell rouses the other keeper from his sleep in time for him to make his toilet. This is a very simple matter on Minot's Ledge—at least in winter. It does not take a man long to put on his clothes there, because, on account of the dampness and cold of the sleeping-rooms, he usually goes to bed with most of his clothes on. I remember one night, when the tower was "sweating" inside, as it often does in winter, we divested ourselves only of jackets and shoes, piled sheets, blankets, and quilts over us, and even then had difficulty in keeping thoroughly warm. I have referred to the bucket which stood under the store-room window to receive water which might drip from the sill. A bucket stands under every window in the tower. The windows on the northeast side are always kept closed in winter, and the heavy wooden shutters bolted, yet the seas strike the tower with such searching power that it was found necessary to run a little gutter along each sill, and to lead a rubber tube from it into the pail; and during severe storms the pails on the weather side often require emptying once an hour. No one thinks of going to bed on Minot's Ledge in winter without a cap or other warm head-covering.

By the time one is dressed—if putting on one's shoes and jacket can be called dressing—

and has washed in the icy water from the well in the granite base, the breakfast is steaming on the table; and a very good breakfast it usually is, for Minot's Ledge is bountifully stocked with provisions. Good food and a pipe of good tobacco are the only luxuries that tend to ameliorate life in this tower.

Breakfast over, and the dishes washed (neatness is of course scrupulously observed), the lamp is trimmed and polished, the lens wiped, and the lantern cleaned. As regards the lamp-chimney, if you ask a lighthouse-keeper the best way to wash lamp-chimneys, he will tell you the best way is not to wash them at all. Rubbing with a dry cloth is the correct method. There is considerable brass-work about the lamp to keep as bright as a mirror, and the care of the lens is a delicate matter. To those whose idea of a lens is derived from a camera or a telescope, the lens which surrounds a lighthouse lamp will be a novelty. It is a veritable structure in itself, consisting of rings of glass, many of them prismatic, built around the lantern. In a second-order light like Minot's, the lens stands four feet high. Not a breath must dim the clearness of

CLEANING THE LANTERN, OUTSIDE.

this beautiful glass-work, which on a bright day reflects all the hues of the rainbow, and at night causes the lamp to cast its grateful rays fifteen and a half miles out to sea.

Cleaning the lantern is at times an arduous

task, and not infrequently a perilous one. The spray is apt to freeze
upon it, and no matter how savagely the gale may be blowing,
the keepers are obliged to brave
it outside upon the lantern-deck,
nearly ninety feet above the sea,
while washing the ice off the glass
with glycerin. As the upper part
of the lantern cannot be reached
from the deck, it is necessary
for the keepers to stand upon
the narrow rail of the parapet and, leaning forward,
grasp an iron support with
one hand, while washing the
glass with a cloth in the
other. The cold and danger
to which the keeper is exposed while performing this
task during a winter gale
can readily be imagined. A
misstep would precipitate
him into the riotous sea far
below.

When lamp, lens, and
lantern have been clean-
ed, and the yellow shades
inside the lantern low-
ered, the lens is care-
fully covered with
a white cloth, and
the keepers do
chores, such
as mak-
ing their
beds,

renovating the white paint on the brick lining,
and putting on necessary little touches here and
there to maintain the scrupulous neatness of the
premises which is embraced within the meaning
of the phrase "keeping a good light." That is
the test by which a lighthouse-keeper stands or
falls. It means that he must not only get out
of the lenticular apparatus and its accessories
in his care a ray that will pierce the darkness as
far as the full capacity of the apparatus will
permit, but also that he must keep the premises
in perfect order. The *esprit de corps* that pre-
vails in the lighthouse service is well illustrated by the fact that the keepers of the first
tower on Minot's Ledge "kept a good light"
up to the moment the tower was overwhelmed
by the sea.

The leisure hours are spent in the watch-
room. In size it is little more than a cell, but
it has the advantage over the rooms below that
it receives daylight through the lee port-hole
and through a manhole in the ceiling leading
to the lantern-deck. It is ten feet in diameter,
but not even all of this small space can be utilized. There are a manhole in the floor for the
stairway from below, the stairs to the lantern-
deck, the columnar support of the lamp, which
takes up the center of the room, and at one side
the incased machinery for striking the fog-bell,
which stands on the parapet outside. Add to
these a stove, two chairs, and a high, shallow
desk, and it may easily be realized that there
is little moving room left. On the desk is the
lighthouse journal, which takes the place of the
log-book on a vessel. Herein are noted the
visits of the inspector, the coming and going
of the keepers, and similar details. You may
also read such entries as:

"Broke ice from lantern. Tower heavily iced
up. . . . A lonesome, snowy day."

The present keeper does not enter items
like the last. "Every day here is lonesome,"
he said, "so that I might just as well enter,
'A lonesome, sunny day.'"

An entry that tells of breaking ice from the
lantern and of the icing up of the tower is usually made after a heavy northeaster — one
of those storms during which the lighthouse
is so completely buried by the heavy seas
that from the shore the tower by day and the
light by night are invisible, except perhaps
at fitful intervals; and the keepers' families
take turns standing watch at the windows
of the dwellings, fearful of a repetition of
the calamity of April, 1851. During such
storms the heavy seas strike the tower about
twenty feet above the base with such force
as to send tons of spray some twenty-five feet
above the dome, — or over a hundred feet
into the air, — and the great mass, not losing its onward rush, comes crashing down

THE ACCIDENT TO THE KEEPER.

upon the lantern, and streams over it on to the parapet and into the ocean beyond. Hanging from davits on this side, with some ninety feet of rope coiled near each davit, is a small life-boat. Though it is swung eighty feet above the sea, it would be dashed to pieces against the parapet if it were on the weather side. Even as it is, the water pours into the boat with such force that it would probably be broken from the davits were it not kept unplugged.

I shall never forget my sensation when the first heavy sea struck the tower during my stay there last February. I was sitting with the assistant keeper in the watch-room. Both of us were reading. At the head of three of the staircases in the tower are heavy iron doors. Suddenly there was a clangorous shock, as if these ponderous doors had crashed to in unison, and a moment later all the demons of the storm seemed to be let loose around the top of the tower, such was the confused roar of wind and water above and about us, the only rhythmic sound being the dismal striking of the fog-bell. " She 's taking on a sea," was all the keeper said. After one of these storms the tower is covered with ice, and tons of it hang from the side of the parapet. As the weather moderates, heavy pieces break off with a loud report, and plunge into the ocean.

Even in perfectly calm weather sounds of the sea eighty feet below rise to the watch-room. The store-room door is kept open as much as possible for ventilation, and the swash of the waves around the foot of the tower travels up through the five stories to the watch-room like a long-drawn gurgle. This, varied with the turmoil of the storm, is all the keepers of Minot's Ledge hear in winter besides their own voices. About their only diversions are reading, and playing games, like cards and draughts, and of these they naturally weary. Even in playing games they cannot make themselves comfortable; for as there is no space for a table in the watch-room, they are obliged to stand up to the bell-casing. " The trouble with our life here," said the keeper, "is that we have too much time to think." Not many years ago one keeper thought so much that he left the watch-room, went below, and cut his throat. Instances when keepers new to life on Minot's have been so frightened by the shock of only moderately heavy seas against the tower that they have left it the first chance possible, have not been uncommon. " No money 'll hire me to stay on Minot's," exclaimed one of these deserters, as he followed his gripsack down the line into the boat.

On the lantern-deck above the watch-room is a spy-glass, and frequently the keepers train this glass upon their dwellings ashore. The principal keeper has children who are attend-

ing school, and at the hour for their leaving or returning home he will invariably be found glass in hand in the lantern or on the parapet. In some respects this proximity to shore adds to the loneliness of life on Minot's. The keepers see what they crave constantly before them without being able to attain it. If, for instance, the keeper's children go to or return from school at some unusual hour, and he misses seeing them, he worries until he catches

THE FOG-BELL.

a glimpse of them again. The keepers are also alarmed if they see a small boat putting out from shore in winter time, apprehensive that it means bad news from home.

Pacing the parapet is the only outdoor exercise Minot's Ledge affords. It may readily be imagined that neither a tennis-court nor a base-ball diamond can be laid out on it. It is a few feet in width, and encircles a room only ten feet in diameter. One cannot walk clear around because the fog-bell obstructs the passage on one side, and in winter the gale is usually so savage that one dare not venture on the weather side.

During my stay at Minot's I often went out on the parapet at night, and peered over the rail into the blackness below me, out of which issued the voice of the sea. There was something indescribably grand in this surging of the unseen ocean. One night, after a gray, threatening day, as I was standing upon the parapet, I heard a sudden rush of wind, and through the halo that surrounded the lantern there scurried what seemed to be myriads of white, ghost-like birds without a twitter or even the rustle of a feather, driven before the storm, and vanishing into the darkness as suddenly as they had emerged from it. Cold, feathery flakes blown into my face told me that this weird effect was produced by a snow-squall whirling around the tower. Another night, as I came out upon the parapet, I was startled to find the sky ribbed with black lines that formed the framework of a huge dome centering directly above the tower. A fog had closed in, and against it were projected the vastly elongated shadows of the iron supports that run from the lantern-deck to the dome above it, while the light, as it was thrown upon the fog by the lens, filled in the spaces with a dun glare that was unearthly in its effect.

The boat that swings from the parapet eighty feet above the sea is lowered only in emergencies. It is remembered of a former keeper that when a small craft was capsized near the tower, he leaped into the lighthouse boat, cast off the lines, and let it descend at full speed. Fortunately, neither cable fouled, otherwise the boat would have remained hanging, stern or bow up, as the case might have been, and the keeper would have been dashed to pieces on the rocks; for, as it was low tide, the ledge was not wholly submerged. At one time a dory was swung from the parapet. While a keeper was letting himself down in it the wood-work in the bow gave way, and the dory hung by its stern, the keeper falling from a great height headlong into the water. Luckily it was flood-tide, but he struck with such force that he penetrated the water far enough to feel the seaweed on the rocks, and he suffers from the effects of the shock to this day. It was discovered that some one had tampered with the dory — with the purpose, it is supposed, of creating a vacancy in the lighthouse service, repulsive as the thought may be.

There are four keepers at Minot's Ledge, or, to be more exact, one keeper and three assistants. They alternate two and two on the tower every fortnight, excepting when stormy weather forbids a landing at the ledge. Keepers have been storm-bound there seven weeks, and when the storm abated sufficiently for them to be lowered by the rope, have discovered, when the boat came out for them, that the door was so heavily iced up they would be unable to open it for several days. It may seem that, with every other fortnight ashore, the keepers of Minot's Ledge have an undue proportion of vacation. But as a matter of fact the two weeks on the tower drag like two years, while the two weeks ashore glide by like two hours. The time ashore is not a holiday, for there is much work to be done about the dwellings and grounds. Yet the position of keeper or assistant on Minot's Ledge is eagerly sought for — by those who have never tried it. Were I asked after my experience on Minot's Ledge to define a sea-rock lighthouse, I should reply, " A prison surrounded by water."

The keepers' dwellings are prettily situated on the Cohasset shore. In an emergency the men on the tower set a signal, in response to which the keepers on shore put off in a small boat. Several days elapsed after I had finished my work on Minot's Ledge before the keeper thought the sea had gone down sufficiently to warrant him in setting the signal. By the time the boat was half-way out the waves had roughened up so that he was obliged to lower the signal, and the little craft turned back. I was detained for three days longer before the boat, after the fourth attempt to reach the tower, succeeded in taking me off by means of the block and tackle. No wonder that days before their tour of duty on the tower ends, the keepers anxiously watch every change of the weather. I experienced the sensation of joy that must thrill through them when they reach shore, when at last I sprang from the gunwale of the little boat to *terra firma.*

Passing up the road that led to the village, I turned as it wound away from the shore for a last look out to sea. On a rocky slope near the dwellings stood one of the keepers, spy-glass in hand. About him, and looking anxiously seaward, was a group of women and children. Beyond the low land of the little harbor the sea was boiling over innumerable rocks and ledges. Against the background of ominous storm-clouds stood the gray tower, the waves, as they dashed against it, tossing the spray high up toward the parapet, from which only a few hours before I had watched the keepers' boat put out from shore. Such was my last glimpse of Minot's Ledge Lighthouse.

SWALLOW-TAIL LIGHT.

Lighthouse, Atlantic City, N. J.

POINT ARENA LIGHT-HOUSE.

NEVERSINK HIGHLANDS LIGHT-HOUSES.

Montauk Point

THE LIGHTSHIP.

LIFE ON THE SOUTH SHOAL LIGHTSHIP.

by Gustav Kobbe

NO. 1, Nantucket, New South Shoal, pitches and plunges, rears and rolls, year in and year out, twenty-four miles off Sankaty Head, Nantucket Island, with the broad ocean to the eastward, and rips and breakers to the westward, northward, and southward. No. 1, Nantucket, New South Shoal, is a lightship—the most desolate and dangerous station in the United States lighthouse establishment. Upon this tossing island, out of sight of land, exposed to the fury of every tempest, and without a message from home during all the stormy months of winter, and sometimes even longer, ten men, braving the perils of wind and wave, and the worse terrors of isolation, trim the lamps whose light warns thousands of vessels from certain destruction, and hold themselves ready to save life when the warning is vain. When vessels have been driven helplessly upon the shoals over which the South Shoal Lightship stands guard, her crew have not hesitated to lower their boat in seas which threatened every moment to stave or to engulf it, and to pull, often in the teeth of a furious gale, to the rescue of the shipwrecked, not only saving their lives but afterward sharing with them, often to their own great discomfort, such cheer as the lightship affords. Yet who ever heard of a medal being awarded

to the life-savers of No. 1, Nantucket, New South Shoal?

Before we left Nantucket for the lightship I gleaned from casual remarks made by grizzled old salts who had heard of our proposed expedition that I might expect something different from a cruise under summer skies. The captain's watch of five men happened to be ashore on leave, and when I called on the captain and told him I had chartered a tug to take Mr. Taber and myself out to the lightship and to call for me a week later, he said, with a pleasant smile, "You've arranged to be called for in seven days, but you can congratulate yourself if you get off in seven weeks." As he gave me his flipper at the door he made this parting remark: "When you set foot on Nantucket again, after you 've been to the lightship, *you will be pleased.*" Another old whaling captain told me that the loneliest thing he had ever seen at sea was a polar bear floating on a piece of ice in the Arctic Ocean; the next loneliest object to that had been the South Shoal Lightship. But the most cheering comment on the expedition was made by an ex-captain of the Cross Rip Lightship, which is anchored in Nantucket Sound in full sight of land, and is not nearly so exposed or desolate a station as the South Shoal. He said very deliberately and solemnly, " If it were n't for the disgrace it would bring on my family I 'd rather go to State's prison." I was also told of times when the South Shoal Lightship so pitched and rolled that even an old whaleman who had served on her seventeen years, and had before that made numerous whaling voyages, felt " squamish," which is the sailor fashion of intimating that even the saltiest old salt is apt to experience symptoms of *mal de mer* aboard a lightship. Life on a lightship therefore presented itself to us as a term of solitary confinement combined with the horrors of sea-sickness.

The South Shoal Lightship being so far out at sea, and so dangerous of approach, owing to the shoals and rips which extend all the way out to her from Nantucket, and which would be fatal barriers to large vessels, the trip can be made only in good weather. That is the reason the crew are cut off so long in winter from communication with the land. The lighthouse tender does not venture out to the vessel at all from December to May, only occasionally utilizing a fair day and a smooth sea to put out far enough just to sight the lightship and to report her as safe at her station. The tender is a little, black side-wheel craft called the *Verbena*, and is a familiar sight to shipping which pass through the Vineyard Sound; but during long months the crew of the South Shoal Lightship see their only connecting link between their lonely ocean home and their firesides ashore loom up only a moment against the wintry sky, to vanish again, leaving them to their communion with the waves and gulls, awakening longings which strong wills had kept dormant, and intensifying the bitterness of their desolation.

The day on which we steamed out of Nantucket Harbor on the little tug *Ocean Queen*, bound for the lightship, the sky was a limpid, luminous, unruffled blue, and the sea a succession of long, lazy swells; yet before we reached our destination we encountered one of the dangers which beset this treacherous coast. We had dropped the lighthouse on Sankaty Head and were eagerly scanning the horizon ahead of us, expecting to raise the lightship, when a heavy fog-bank spread itself out directly in our course. Soon we were in it. Standing on until we should have run our distance, we stopped and blew our whistle. The faint tolling of a bell answered us through the fog. Plunging into the mist in the direction from which the welcome sound seemed to come, we steamed for about half an hour and then, coming to a stop, whistled again. There was no answer. Signal after signal remained without reply. Again we felt our way for a while, and again whistled. This time we heard the bell once more, but only to lose it as before. Three times we heard it, and three times lost it, and, as the fog was closing in thick about us, it seemed hopeless for us to continue our search any longer at the risk of losing the opportunity of putting back to shore before nightfall and the possible com-

ing up of a blow. Then, more than three hours after we had first heard the bell, it rang out to windward clearer and stronger than before. Then there loomed out of the fog the vague outlines of a vessel. There was a touch of the weird in this apparition. Flying mist still veiled it, and prevented its lines from being sharply defined. It rode over the waves far out at sea, a blotch of brownish red with bare masts; and the tide, streaming past it out of some sluice between the shoals, made it appear as if it were scurrying along without a rag set —a Flying Dutchman, to add to the terrors of reefs and rips. The weirdness of the scene was not dispelled until we were near enough to read in bold white letters on the vessel's side No. 1, Nantucket, New South Shoal. After groping around in the fog, and almost despairing of finding the object of our search, we felt as we steamed up to the lightship, a wonderful sense of relief, and realized the feeling of joy with which the sight of her must inspire the mariner who is anxiously on the lookout for some beacon by which to shape his course.

Two days later we had what was perhaps a more practical illustration of the lightship's usefulness. It was a hazy morning, and the mate was scanning the horizon with his glass. Bringing it to bear to the southward, he held it long in that direction, while a look of anxiety came over his face. Several of the crew joined him and finally one of them said, " If she keeps that course five minutes longer she 'll be on the shoal." Through the haze a large three-masted schooner was discernible, heading directly for a reef to the southwest of us. She was evidently looking for the lightship, but the haze had prevented her from sighting us, although our sharp lookout had had his glass on her for some time. Then too, as the mate remarked with a slightly critical smile, " These captains feel so sure of their course that they always expect to raise us straight ahead." Suddenly there was evidence that she had sighted us. She swung around as swiftly as if she were turning upon a pivot. She had been lunging along in an uncertain way, but the sight of us seemed to fill her with new life and buoyancy. Her sails filled, she dashed through the waves with streaks of white streaming along each quarter like foam on the flanks of a race-horse, and on she came, fairly quivering with joy from keel to pennant. Such instances are of almost daily occurrence, and if we add to them the occasions — and they must run far up into the hundreds, if not into the thousands — when the warning voice of the fog-bell and the guiding gleam of the lamps have saved vessels from shipwreck, it seems as though the sailor must look upon the South Shoal Lightship as one of the guardian angels of the deep.

A HAZY MORNING.

Only the peculiarly dangerous character of the coast could have warranted the Government in placing a lightship in so exposed a position. Nantucket is a veritable ocean graveyard. There are records of over five hundred disasters to vessels on its shores and outlying reefs. How many ships, hidden by fog or sleet one hundred and three feet long over all, with twenty-four feet breadth of beam, and stanchly built of white and live oak. She has two hulls, the space between them being filled through holes at short intervals in the inner side of the bulwarks with salt—"to keep her sweet," as the nautical paradox runs. These holes are closed

TAKING IN THE LIGHT.

from the watchers on shore and never heard from, have been lost on the latter, is a question to which the sea will never give answer; but many a poor fellow whose end has remained a mystery to anxious hearts at home has laid his bones upon the sands of the Nantucket shoals, which are a constant menace both to coasters taking the outside route for New England and Dominion ports and to European shipping, which shapes its course for New York after sighting the South Shoal Lightship. This vessel, therefore, stands guard not only over the New South Shoal, near which it is anchored, but over twenty-four miles of rips and reefs between it and the shore of Nantucket.

It has been on this station since 1856. A lightship was placed on the Old South Shoal, some miles farther in, during 1855; but its cable parted in one of the winter storms, and the vessel was wrecked on Montauk. Meanwhile the New South Shoal had been discovered, and the new lightship was anchored some two miles to the southeast of it. The shoal itself is marked by a red buoy.

No. 1, Nantucket, New South Shoal, is a schooner of two hundred and seventy-five tons, by black plugs which are attached to the bulwarks by short bits of tarred rope, and the line of plugs running the length of the vessel forms a series of black dots near the rail which at once strikes the eye as a distinguishing mark between this and other ships. She is fore-and-aft lantern-masts seventy-one feet high, including topmasts, and directly behind each of the lantern-masts a mast for sails forty-two feet high. Forty-four feet up the lantern-masts are day-marks, reddish brown hoop-iron gratings, which enable other vessels to sight the lightship more readily. The lanterns are octagons of glass in copper frames five feet in diameter, four feet nine inches high, with the masts as centers. Each pane of glass is two feet long and two feet three inches high. There are eight lamps, burning a fixed white light, with parabolic reflectors in each lantern, which weighs, all told, about a ton. Some nine hundred gallons of oil are taken aboard for service during the year. The lanterns are lowered into houses built around the masts. The house around the main lantern-mast stands directly on the deck, while the foremast lantern-house is a heavily timbered frame three feet high.

THE SOUTH SHOAL LIGHTSHIP.

This is to prevent its being washed away by the waves the vessel ships when she plunges into the wintry seas. When the lamps have been lighted and the roofs of the lantern-houses opened,— they work on hinges, and are raised by tackle,— the lanterns are hoisted by means of winches to a point about twenty-five feet from the deck. Were they to be hoisted higher they would make the ship top-heavy.

A conspicuous object forward is the large fog-bell swung ten feet above the deck. The prevalence of fog makes life on the South Shoal Lightship especially dreary. During one season fifty-five days out of seventy were thick, and for twelve consecutive days and nights the bell was kept tolling at two-minute intervals, until the crew became so used to its iron voice that when the fog lifted they had to accustom themselves to getting along without it, the silence actually disturbing their sleep the first night. Shackled to the keelson is a chain of two-inch thickness, which runs through a deck-pipe to the deck and over the latter forward to a hawse-pipe, through which it runs into the water full one hundred and five fathoms to the "mushroom," an anchor shaped like an inverted saucer and weighing 6500 pounds, which holds the vessel in eighteen fathoms of water. It is difficult to imagine that any power could part a chain of such strength, yet the South Shoal Lightship has been adrift twenty-three times, leaving a regular mushroom plantation at the bottom of the sea around the spot over which she is anchored. On one of these occasions she was fourteen days at sea, and on another she came to anchor in New York harbor. In spite of her two sail-masts she is rather indifferently rigged for such emergencies. Carrying only trysails to the sail-masts, a square-sail to the fore lantern-mast, a forestaysail, and a jib, she cannot beat against the wind, and hence when she parts her cable in an offshore gale she is blown out to sea until the wind shifts to a favorable point.

The most thrilling experience of this kind fell to the lot of the Cross Rip Lightship, which is anchored in Nantucket Sound. Her position is not so exposed or so desolate as the South Shoal, but she happens to have once parted her cable under peculiarly perilous circumstances, no word of her or her crew being received for over a month, when, after both ship and men had been given up for lost, the mate telegraphed the safe arrival of all hands in New Orleans. On the night of December 27, 1867, the captain being ashore, the Cross Rip Lightship took a heavy, icy gale from the southwest and rolled and plunged until one o'clock in the morning, when, the gale having increased to a perfect hurricane, she parted her cable, at the same time shipping a sea that carried away her life-boat. The harbor anchor was then cleared away, the mate giving her the whole of the chain. In spite of the terrible strain, she rode on this chain about ten hours, when she parted it some twenty fathoms from the anchor. The wind was then directly from the west. With her small sail area and her bow heavily weighted by the chains she was dragging, the handling of her was a difficult matter. There was not a cold chisel aboard with which the chains could be cleared away, for, owing to the frequent parting of the South Shoal, the Lighthouse Board suspected the crew of having tampered with the cable and had adopted rigorous measures to prevent any one taking a cold chisel aboard a lightship.

About one o'clock in the afternoon the lighthouse on Great Point, Nantucket, was made,

and the mate endeavored to beach the vessel; but finding she would go on the rip, he wore ship and stood out to sea. At three o'clock the mainsail split, and an examination showed four feet of water in the lower hold. She was fairly sheathed with ice, which had to be cleared away from around the pump before the men could get to work at the latter. At eignt o'clock that night the foresail split, and, with a gale still blowing and a heavy sea running, there was nothing to do but to keep the pumps manned to prevent the ship, which was now at the mercy of wind and waves, from sinking. At eight o'clock on the morning of the 30th the crew were nearly exhausted, and the water had gained so that the vessel was settling. In this predicament, rendered more desperate by the loss of the boat, which left them absolutely without means of saving themselves, a sail was sighted to windward. The colors were set union down, and three hours later a vessel, which proved to be bound for New Orleans, spoke the distressed light-ship, and, lowering a boat, took off the crew. They were saved just in time. Before they sailed out of sight the Cross Rip Lightship took her last plunge.

The South Shoal, like all lightships, is very high in the bow and heavily timbered—built to stay and built to kill. A lightship is in frequent danger of collision from other vessels, and as its preservation is of such importance to shipping interests it is constructed so that of the two ships it will be the one to survive the shock. Life aboard a lightship is in itself so desolate that the men's quarters are made as roomy as possible. The captain and the mate have a pleasant cabin aft, with two staterooms, a large table, lockers, and the ship library, a small case of miscellaneous books supplied by the Lighthouse Board. It cannot be said of the South Shoal's crew that they make much use of the library. About the only book aboard that looks well thumbed is a little pamphlet giving a record of the vessels that have met with disaster on the Nantucket coast. This is often referred to as an authority in settling disputes regarding the date and circumstances of certain wrecks. A door leads from the cabin into the berth-deck, which occupies the space usually taken for the upper hold. On each side are bunks which slope in towards the middle so that their occupants will not be thrown out by the violent rolling and lurching of the ship. In front of these bunks are the men's chests, which they also use for seats. Forward on the berth-deck is the cooking-stove and beyond it the mess-table. The lightship version of the "dinner under difficulties," familiar to every ocean traveler, is, if anything, a little livelier than the original. The method of keeping the table

THE FOG-BELL.

service in place is, however, somewhat more primitive than that in use on the ocean greyhounds. There are holes in the table into which pegs are fitted, and around each dish and cup is a little fence of these pegs. Sometimes, however, a plate will clear the fence on a running jump and deposit its contents in a dish of quite a different character, the result being a conglomeration mysterious enough to puzzle even a person who has solved the most profound problems of the culinary art. The mainstays of life aboard a lightship are scouse and duff.

Scouse is a wonderful commingling of salt beef, potatoes, and onions, with varied trimmings. Duff seems substantially like the dumplings served in Yorkshire pudding with a sauce of melted brown sugar. Plum duff—with raisins —is a great luxury; but often the plums are nothing more than "Nantucket raisins"—in plain English, dried apples. Now it is easy to imagine the result if a rolling sea causes the scouse and the duff, with its sugary sauce, to fraternize. The cook's duties on the South Shoal are performed under similar difficulties. So vehement is the pitching and rolling of the vessel that the pots and kettles are lashed to the stove to prevent them from winging their flight into various corners of the berth-deck. Despite these precautions, however, certain courses have at times been served with unexpected expedition. Thus, on one occasion during our stay, the pork made a flying leap from the pot into one of the port bunks, the occupant of which, while gratified at the generous propor-

remarkably long time when the desolate character of the service is considered. This is probably due to the fact that the dangers of this exposed station warn off all but those inured to the hardships of a seafaring life. The men who have been there so long are old whalemen, accustomed to voyages of several years' duration and to the perils of a whaleman's life. The pay aboard the South Shoal is somewhat higher than on other lightships. The captain receives

HOT COFFEE.

tions of the ration, expressed his preference for a service less automatic and rapid.

The routine of work on a lightship is quite simple. At sunrise the watch lowers the lights. At six A. M. the captain or the mate stands in the doorway leading from the cabin into the berth-deck and shouts, "All hands!" The men tumble out of their bunks and dress, breakfast being served at twenty minutes past six. At half-past seven the lamps are removed from the lanterns and taken below to be cleaned and filled. In smooth weather this duty can be performed in about two hours, but if the vessel is rolling and pitching the task may be prolonged an hour or two. When the lamps have been returned to the lanterns there remains nothing for the crew to do except to clean ship and to go on watch until sundown, when the lamps are lighted and the lanterns hoisted. The crew is divided into the captain's watch and the mate's watch of five each. Twice between spring and winter each watch goes ashore for two months, so that each member of the crew is aboard the lightship eight months in the year. It is not believed that they could stand the life longer than this. In fact, many men throw up their work as soon as they can get ashore. Three members of the South Shoal crew have, however, seen unusually long terms of service — twenty-one, nineteen, and seventeen years respectively, and others have served on her a

$1000, the mate $700, and the crew $600. These sums may not seem large, but it must be borne in mind that even the prodigal son would have found it impossible to make way with his patrimony on the South Shoal Lightship, especially as the Government furnishes all supplies. Opportunities for extravagance are absolutely wanting. Occasionally a member of the crew may remark in a sadly jocose tone that he is going around the corner to order a case of champagne or to be measured for a dress-suit; but there is no corner.

A number of stores in Nantucket sell what are known as lightship-baskets. They come in "nests," a nest consisting of five or eight baskets of various sizes fitting one into the other. These baskets are made only on the South Shoal Lightship. Their manufacture has been attempted ashore, but has never paid. This is because there is a very narrow margin of profit in them for the lightship crew, who make them chiefly for the purpose of whiling away the weary winter hours. In summer the crew occupies its spare time "scrimshawing," an old whaling term for doing ingenious mechanical work, but having aboard the South Shoal the special meaning of preparing the strips of wood and ratan for the manufacture of the baskets in winter. The bottoms are turned ashore. The blocks over which the baskets are made have been aboard the ship since she was first anchored off the New South Shoal in 1856. The sides of the baskets are of white oak or hickory, filled in with ratan, and they are round or oval, of graceful lines and of great durability, the sizes to a nest ranging from a pint to a peck and a half.

But notwithstanding these various attempts at killing time, life on the South Shoal Lightship is at its best a life of desolation, with only a few gulls or Mother Carey's chickens for visitors, who seek refuge aboard in stormy weather. The red buoy bobbing up and down two miles to westward has become almost as much endeared to the crew as if it were a human companion. A man rarely comes up from below without casting a look over the bulwarks to see if the buoy is still there. Fog is dreaded, not only because it throws a pall over the sea and because the dismal tolling of the bell adds to the depression aboard, but also because it hides the buoy from sight; and as the fog recedes all eyes anxiously scan the horizon until the bonny buoy looms up out of the mist. As the ship swings around a good deal with wind and tide, the buoy marks a fixed

towards them from over the sea; and when the mirage melted away, and they felt again that twenty-four miles of ocean rolled between them and land, they turned away dejectedly and silently went below. Once, so one of the crew told me next morning, the mirage had been so strong that they had seen Nantucket plainly enough to discern the dories on Sunset Beach, and that this fleeting sight of land, after they had been exposed for nearly five months to the weary life of the lightship, had so intensified their longing for home that they were dejected enough to have been a set of castaways on a desert island, without hope of ever laying eyes on their native shores.

The emotional stress under which this crew labors can hardly be realized by any one who has not been through a similar experience. The sailor on an ordinary ship has at least the inspiration of knowing that he is bound for somewhere; that in due time his vessel will be laid on her homeward course; that storm and fog are but incidents of the voyage: he is on a ship that leaps forward full of life and energy

CLEANING THE LAMPS.

point of the compass for the crew, and thus the men have grown to regard it with a feeling of affectionate reliance. When that buoy parts and drifts away, as it sometimes does, the crew seem as depressed as if they had lost their only friend in the world.

One night when I was on deck the mate, who had the watch, rushed to the hatch and shouted down into the berth-deck, "Sankaty!" It seemed but an instant before the entire crew had scrambled up the gangway and were crowded at the bulwarks watching the light from Nantucket's grandest headland flash out

with every lash of the tempest. But no matter how the lightship may plunge and roll, no matter how strong the favoring gales may be, she is still anchored two miles southeast of the New South Shoal.

Those who endeavor to form an idea of the motion of the South Shoal Lightship must remember that she is as much at the mercy of the waves as a vessel stripped of sails or deprived of motive power in mid-ocean. Even in smooth weather the motion is entirely different from that of a ship under way. For a few minutes she will lie on an even keel, and

A RESCUE.

then without warning she will roll so that the water streams in through her scuppers. In the expressive language of her captain, "She washes her own decks." For this reason the port-holes of the cabin and the berth-deck are never opened, she being liable at any moment to swing around into the trough of the sea and to roll so as to take in water at them. In winter the violence of the pitching and rolling is such as to try the hardihood of the men to the utmost. On one occasion she rolled so sheer to starboard that she filled the starboard life-boat, which was swung high on davits, and then rolled so sheer to port that the boat emptied itself down the hatch into the berth-deck, drenching every one.

In winter, when the rigging begins tuning up until it fairly shrieks like a gigantic æolian harp at the touch of the hurricane, the poor fellow who, while dreaming of home, is awakened to take his turn at the watch on deck is exposed to the full fury of the elements. Then the ship, being unable to "use herself," butts at the waves so that the bow is submerged one moment and the boom the next, while the spray flies like a "living smoke" all over her, sheathing even the masts to the height of fifty feet with ice. At times the water and spray freeze so quickly upon her that the ice extends for twelve feet or more on each side of the bow, and a thick layer of it covers her deck, while the bulwarks are built up with it until holes have to be chopped through it to enable the crew to look out to sea. It also forms to the thickness of a barrel around the rigging. In fact, it has covered the ship so completely that not a splinter of wood could be seen. In some seasons the severest storms have burst over the vessel about Christmas time, so that on Christmas eve each man has passed his watch standing forward on the icy deck pulling at the rope of the lightship bell, with the wind shrieking in the stays, the spray dashing over him, and sleet drifting wildly about him. What a celebration of the most joyous festival of the year, with the thought of wife and children ashore!

Besides enduring the hardships incidental to their duties aboard the lightship, the South Shoal crew have done noble work in saving life. While the care of the lightship is considered of such importance to shipping that the crew are instructed not to expose themselves to dangers outside their special line of duty, and they would therefore have the fullest excuse for not risking their lives in rescuing others, they have never hesitated to do so. When, a few winters ago, the *City of Newcastle* went ashore on one of the shoals near the lightship and strained herself so badly that although she floated off she soon filled and went down stern foremost, all hands, twenty-seven in number, were saved by the South Shoal crew and kept aboard of her over two weeks, until the story of the wreck was signaled to some passing vessel and the lighthouse tender took them off. This is the largest number saved at one time by the South Shoal, but the lightship crew have faced greater danger on several other occasions. One stormy morning about the middle of January the watch descried a small, dark object over the water several miles to windward, and drifting rapidly away on the strong tide. The captain, on examining it through the glass, thought he perceived signs of life. In spite of the heavy sea that threatened every moment to stave the life-boat, it was lowered, and the crew pulled in the teeth of the furious gale towards the object. As they drew nearer they made out a man feebly waving a cloth. A full view, as they came up, disclosed the evidence of an ocean tragedy. Here, driven before wind and tide, and at the mercy of a winter storm, was a small raft. Stretched upon it was a corpse, held fast by the feet, which had caught under the boom. On the corpse sat a man, his face buried in his hands, and nearly dead with exposure. The man who had waved to them stood upon the grating holding himself upright by a rope which, fastened at two ends of the raft, passed over his shoulder. Having taken the two men who were still alive into the boat, the captain of the South Shoal at once asked them what disposition he should make of the corpse. Being, like all sailors, superstitious, he was unwilling to take the dead body into the boat and bury it from the South Shoal, lest it should sink directly under the lightship and bring ill luck upon her. The poor fellow's shipmates agreed that he should be given over to the sea then and there. So the captain, raising his voice above the storm, pronounced a verse of Scripture, and, drawing the corpse's feet from under the boom, allowed it to slide off the raft. But the sleeves of the dead man's oilers, having filled with air, prevented him from sinking, and, as it would have been a bad omen had he been allowed to float, one of the lightship crew slit the sleeves, and the waves closed over the frozen body of poor Jack. Often vessels lie to near the lightship for provisions and water, and during the war, when the Confederate cruiser *Tallahassee* destroyed the fishing fleet on St. George's Bank, three of the crews, rather than be made prisoners, took to their boats and pulled all the way in to the South Shoal.

It might be supposed that after the crew have been subjected to the desolation of a winter twenty-four miles out at sea, their hearts would bound with joy when the *Verbena* heaves in sight in the spring. But the sight of her is as apt to raise the anxious thought, " What news does she bring from home ? "

But after all is said of the hardships endured by the crew of No. 1, Nantucket, New South Shoal, the fact remains that the men are about as hale a looking set of fellows as one can find anywhere. Then, too, they at times discover in very gratifying ways that their vocation is appreciated. A fruiterer may lie to long enough to transfer to the lightship a welcome gift of bananas or oranges, and not infrequently passing vessels signal their readiness to take the crew's mail off the ship and to forward it from port.

The lightship's utter isolation from other parts of the world is, from certain points of view, a great hardship, but from others it has its advantages. When there is a heavy sea running, the view of the ocean as one "lays off" in a warm sun is unrivaled. The proximity of the rips and shoals gives the scene a beauty entirely its own. On every shoal there glistens at regular intervals the white curve of a huge breaker. Sunsets can be witnessed from the deck of this vessel which, if faithfully reproduced on canvas, would be unhesitatingly pronounced the gorgeous offspring of the artist's imagination. I remember one evening when the sun vanished beneath a bank of fog, permeating it with a soft purple light and edging it with a fringe of reddish gold. Right above it the sky melted from a soft green into the lovely blue that still lingered from the glorious day. Overhead the clouds were whipped out in shreds of fiery yellow, while in all directions around the ship was an undulating expanse of rose-colored sea. Gradually the colors faded away ; the creaking of the winches, as the crew raised the lanterns, broke upon the evening silence ; two pathways of light streamed over the waves — and No. 1, Nantucket, New South Shoal, was ready to stand guard for another night.

TIRED OUT.

HIGHLAND LIGHT, CAPE COD.

Lighthouse, Sanibel Island, Fla.

Long beach bar - Light house

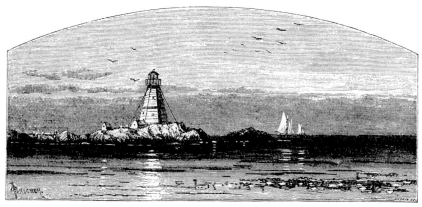

HEAD HARBOR LIGHT.

LIGHT-HOUSE, FERNANDINA.

Off Fire Island, New York.

BAR LIGHT-HOUSE, MOUTH OF ST. JOHN'S RIVER.

HEROISM IN THE LIGHTHOUSE SERVICE.

A DESCRIPTION OF LIFE ON MATINICUS ROCK.

by Gustav Kobbe

WITH PICTURES BY W. TABER.

N two articles of mine which have appeared in THE CEN-TURY — «Life on the South Shoals Light-p» and «Life on a Lighthouse (Minot's lge)»—I have given instances of hero-i displayed in the United States light-se service. The Nantucket light-ship, the South Shoals is now called, has been ored even farther out than when I was ard her. Her crew displays that qual-of heroism which appeals most forcibly the heart and the imagination, the un-scious, every-day heroism of those who ve on the deep; for mere service on this it-station, the most exposed in the world, ooses a strain upon the mental, moral, and rsical stamina of the men which even a g and dangerous voyage does not involve. their heroism is not passive. Though not iged,—in fact, though cautioned against ning any risk to save life, for fear their ı ship might be left short-handed in case lisaster to themselves,—they have never hesitated to lower away and hasten to the rescue of the shipwrecked.

The most noted instance of heroism in the lighthouse service was, however, the devotion to duty of the two assistant keepers of the first Minot's Ledge lighthouse, which was destroyed in the great storm of April, 1851. These men—one a German, the other a «Portugee»—«kept a good light» until it was extinguished by the rising sea, in which they themselves soon after lost their lives.

When the Sharp's Island light in Chesapeake Bay was carried away by ice, the keepers, though they could have abandoned it and made sure of their own safety, tended the light to the last, and clung to the structure, so that when they were rescued, after many hours of peril, they were able to report that they had saved a large portion of the valuable apparatus.

Some of the most picturesque light-stations in the United States lighthouse establishment are on the rocks and islands off the coast of Maine. The ever-surging ocean; the fissured granite, seaweed-stained and tide-marked; the overhanging pines, gnarled and wind-whipped into fantastic shapes, impart a wild beauty to these sites. The towers which stand thereon are among our oldest coast lights, are built of granite the hard gray of which has been softly darkened by age, and are of the old-fashioned type which the lover of the sea always associates with the idea of a lighthouse. Rising with an antique grace from among their picturesque environs, they seem peculiarly fitted to shed their light like a benediction upon the waves.

About a lighthouse which even among these is conspicuous for its beauty—that on Matinicus Rock—cluster a number of incidents which give it peculiar interest. Life there is, as it has been for many years, a constant struggle of human nature against the elements which seek to wear it out. When the lighthouse tender was off Matinicus Island, six miles north of the rock, we spied, about half-way across the reach, a dory laboring in the waves. Our mate, a typical old sea-dog who had braved danger in pretty nearly every part of the Western ocean, remarked, « That fellow has cheek, to be out here in a dory in such a sea!»

As we approached the dory we discovered that one of the assistant keepers of Matinicus Rock was at the oars, while in the bottom sat a girl, warmly wrapped, and utilizing one of the seats as a back-rest. Having taken the dory in tow, we learned that the keeper was bringing his daughter home to the rock from the school which she had been attending at Ragged Island. It was characteristic of the life these people lead—this girl's returning to the rock from school in midwinter, in an open boat across a long reach of ugly sea.

When the *Iris* lay to off the rock we cast

A SOUTHEAST GALE.

ENGRAVED BY M. HAIDER.

loose the dory, and the assistant keeper, having safely landed his daughter, returned with Keeper Grant. There were now stowed in the little craft, besides myself, two of the keeper's nephews. They had passed their boyhood on the rock, and had made use of this chance to revisit their old home. There were thus five people in the dory, besides some baggage.

The landing was sheltered by a rocky ledge which jutted out in such a manner that in order to get behind it the dory was obliged to turn broadside on to the sea. This morning the breakers were executing what was nothing less than a grand flank movement around the southwestern end of the rock, and rushing in upon a ledge a little to the left of the landing. We made the passage safely to the point where it was necessary to turn. For a while we lay stern to the breakers, riding them safely. Then, at what seemed a favorable moment, we turned the little craft. We had, however, pulled only a few strokes when we saw a series of huge breakers flanking the rock and rushing toward us. In vain we tried to slue the dory around to meet them head on. It was too heavily loaded to respond quickly enough. We saw the crest of a breaker towering above us, there was the rush and roar of a deluge, and a moment later the dory was careening over on top of the ledge abreast of which we had been, and we were spilled into the icy water between it and the rock. Had the dory been hurled against the ledge instead of lifted on top of it, the consequences might have been most serious. In fact, it was one of those narrow escapes which are very pleasant to look back upon, but which one would rather not have repeated. As an actual experience of one of the dangers to which the dwellers upon Matinicus Rock are exposed, it was, however, a brilliant success. Keeper Grant's nephews said it made them feel at home again, it was so much like old times. The father of the boys had been an assistant keeper of these lights, while their grandfather on their father's side, and their great-grandfather on their mother's, had been keepers.

The Matinicus Rock light-station stands upon a huge granite rock off the southeastern entrance to Penobscot Bay, Maine, about twenty-two miles out at sea. The rock is some thirty-two acres in size, oblong-shaped, and presents its high southeastern front to the ocean, sloping away toward the northwest. Boulders, strewn in fantastic confusion over its surface, are believed to have been loosened from its front by the destructive force of the sea applied for countless centuries, then lifted during some frenzied outburst, and deposited on top of this cliff-wall, to be gradually moved down the opposite slope when the sea, as not infrequently happens during wintry storms, makes a clean breach over the rock. Not far from the northwestern end is a boulder, the weight of which has been calculated by a stone-cutter to be about a hundred tons, which has been moved twelve feet within the memory of the present keeper, and has been moved nearly a hundred feet if appearances can be trusted. Its pointed top rises high above the surrounding boulders, and after a snow-storm resembles a miniature snow-capped mountain-peak. Where the sea sweeps around the northeastern point

it has formed along the low edge a sea-wall of small, smooth-worn rocks.

The original Matinicus Rock light-station, erected in 1827, was a cobblestone dwelling with a wooden tower at each end. In 1847 these towers were removed, and a granite dwelling with semicircular towers was built. Since then it has developed into an establishment of considerable dimensions, requiring the services of a keeper and three assistants. The granite dwelling still stands, but the present station has two gray granite towers one hundred and eighty feet apart, and connected by a low covered passage; for in high winter storms it would be a hard scramble for the keepers to make their way from tower to tower in the open, not only on account of the wind, which often blows a hurricane, but also because of the heavy seas which break over the rock. Then there are the keepers' dwellings, a brick house with engines for operating two fog-whistles (one held in reserve, in case of accident to that in use), and, as a further precaution, a fog-bell swung from a wooden pyramidal skeleton stand, a brick storehouse for oil, and the boat-house with a timber-way slanting into the water, up which the boats are hoisted by a winch. The towers are ninety-five feet above the sea. The lights, classed as of the third

A BIT OF THE SHORE.

order, are seen fifteen miles away. The rock where the towers stand is fifty feet above the sea, and presents what seems a precipitous front to the ocean. Yet the waves have beaten a sluiceway out of the granite, up which the seas rush, bursting among the boulders, and hurling tons of spray in all directions, or making a clean breach over the rock, the water pouring like a cataract down the northwestern slope, now losing itself among the rocks that are strewn in all directions, now striking one of them, and spouting high into the air, now streaming through some granite trough toward the reach of breakers. The sea has indulged in some curious pranks during these larks. The occupants of a room in the second story of one of the dwellings were awakened one night by a crash of window-glass and a flood of icy water pouring in upon them, and were obliged to flee for safety. The windows had been broken by spray from a wave that had burst among the boulders. A favorite amusement of the ocean was to bowl down the whistle-house, as if intent upon diminishing in some way the efficiency of the station. The old whistle-house stood a little farther forward from the eastern tower than the present structure. That little was just too much. Two buildings on that spot were lifted off their foundations and strewn among the rocks, the boiler being rolled more than a hundred feet. The old foundations, considerably strengthened by a breakwater, now form a guard for the new whistle-house.

Several of the violent storms that have whirled over Matinicus Rock have tried the fortitude of the little band of faithful watchers upon it. One of these watchers, Abby Burgess, has become famous in our light-house annals, not only for long service, but also for bravery displayed on various occasions. Her father was keeper of the rock from 1853 to 1861. In January, 1856, when she was seventeen years old, he left her in charge of the lights while he crossed to Matinicus Island. His wife was an invalid, his son was away on a cruise, and his other four children were little girls. The following day it began to « breeze up »; the wind increased to a gale, and soon developed into a storm almost as furious as that which carried away the tower on Minot's Ledge in 1851. Before long the seas were sweeping over the rock. Down among the boulders was a chicken-coop which Abby feared might be carried away. On a lonely ocean outpost like Matinicus Rock a chicken is regarded with affectionate interest, and Abby, solicitous for the safety of the inmates of the little coop, waited her chance, and when the seas fell off a little rushed knee-deep through the swirling water, and rescued all but one of the chickens. She had hardly closed the door of the dwelling behind her when a sea, breaking over the rock, brought down the old cobblestone house with a crash. While the storm was at its height the waves threatened the granite dwelling, so that the family had to take refuge in the towers for safety; and here they remained, with no sound to greet them from without but the roaring of the

THE BREAKWATER.

ABBY SAVES THE CHICKENS.

ENGRAVED BY ALBERT BLOSSE.

nd around the lanterns, and no sight but e sea sheeting over the rock. Yet through all the lamps were trimmed and lighted. en after the storm abated, the reach be- een the rock and Matinicus Island was so ugh that Captain Burgess could not return til four weeks later.

During a subsequent winter there was so ng a spell of rough weather that pro- ions ran low, and Captain Burgess was liged to utilize the first chance of putting for Matinicus Island, although there was telling how soon the sea might roughen again. In point of fact, a heavy storm oke over the coast before he could return,

and before long there was danger of famine on the rock. In this strait Captain Burgess's son, who happened to be at home, decided to brave the storm in a skiff rigged with a spritsail. A small group of anxious watchers followed the little sail with straining eyes until the storm-scud hid it from sight. Twenty-one days passed before he and his father returned—days of hope alternating with fear, and the hardship of meager fare through all, the daily allowance dwindling to an egg and a cup of corn-meal each, with danger of that short ration giving out if the storm did not abate. During all this time Abby was obliged not only to care for the lights, but also to tend an invalid mother and cheer up the little family in its desolate state.

In 1861 Captain Burgess retired from Ma-

A JIG IN THE KEEPER'S PARLOR.

Grant proved a very apt pupil—so apt that he was soon able not only to take care of the lights, but also to persuade his instructress to let him take care of her. She became his wife and his helpmate in a double sense, for not long after their marriage she was appointed an assistant keeper. When she was married she had lived on the rock eight years, and she remained there until 1875, when her husband was appointed keeper, and she assistant keeper, of the light on White Head, an island separated from Spruce Head only by a narrow channel. Matinicus Rock, twenty-two miles out at sea, with the grand sweep of the ocean, the rough shores of Ragged Island and Matinicus Island and on the west, the dim outlines of Vinal Haven to the north, and in the background the dark, towering forms of the Camden Mountains—this rock, with its wilderness of boulders, its wind, snow, and fog, its shrieking whistle and clanging bell, its loneliness and perils, had been her home for twenty-two years. There

tinicus, Captain Grant and his family succeeding him. And now the grim old wave-rent rock became the scene of as pretty a romance as could be devised. A son of Captain Grant had been appointed assistant to his father, and Captain Burgess had left Abby on the rock to instruct the newcomers in the care of the lights. Young

she had performed the triple duties of wife, mother, and lighthouse-keeper. The transfer to White Head brought some change from the old accustomed surroundings; but the duties, requiring such faithful performance, were the same. The Grants remained fifteen years in charge of White Head. In May, 1890, they removed to Middleborough in Plymouth

County, Massachusetts, expecting to pass the remainder of their lives out of hearing of the turmoil of the sea. Yet life away from it seemed strange and unattractive, and two years later found them again on the coast of Maine, this time at Portland, where the husband had reëntered the lighthouse establishment, working in the Engineers' Department of the First Lighthouse District. With them lives Captain Grant, who in the fall of 1890, at the age of eighty-five, retired from the position of keeper of Matinicus Rock, which he had held for twenty-nine years.

Shortly before leaving White Head Mrs. Grant wrote to a friend:

Sometimes I think the time is not far distant when I shall climb these lighthouse stairs no more. It has almost seemed to me that the light was a part of myself. When we had care of the old lard-oil lamps on Matinicus Rock, they were more difficult to tend than these lamps are, and sometimes they would not burn so well when first lighted, especially in cold weather when the oil got cool. Then, some nights, I could not sleep a wink all night, though I knew the keeper himself was watching. And many nights I have watched the lights my part of the night, and then could not sleep the rest of the night, thinking nervously what might happen should the light fail.

In all these years I always put the lamps in order in the morning and I lit them at sunset. Those old lamps—as they were when my father lived on Matinicus Rock—are so thoroughly impressed on my memory that even now I often dream of them. There were fourteen lamps and fourteen reflectors. When I dream of them it always seems to me that I have been away a long while, and I am trying to get back in time to light the lamps. Then I am half-way between Matinicus and White Head, and hurrying toward the rock to light the lamps there before sunset. Sometimes I walk on the water, sometimes I am in a boat, and sometimes I seem going in the air— I must always see the lights burning in both places before I wake. I always go through the same scenes in cleaning the lamps and lighting them, and I feel a great deal more worried in my dreams than when I am awake.

I wonder if the care of the lighthouse will follow my soul after it has left this worn-out body! If I ever have a gravestone, I would like it to be in the form of a lighthouse or beacon.

Before Captain Grant retired from the rock three of his sons had served under him as assistants, and one of them succeeded him as keeper. But the old rock still has such attractions for the old keeper that he visits it at intervals. The summer he was eighty-seven years old he went mackerel-fishing from the rock, and returned with the largest individual catch to his credit.

His grandchildren, the nephews of the present keeper, who went out with me on the *Iris*, loved every inch of the rock. «Few children who are brought up on the mainland,» said one of them, «have such good times as we had.»

Along the edge of their rocky home, and among the boulders, these boys had roamed so often that what to a casual observer would seem nothing more than reaches of fissured granite and a confused heap of jagged rock had assumed for them that variety of form and feature which we would look for in a highly diversified landscape. Every little indentation became a cove, every little pool among the rocks a pond, and for these miniature topographical features they had names like Spear Point, Western Guzzle, Devil's Gulch, Fort George, Canoe Pond; while a mass of boulders became the Rocky Mountains of this thirty-two acres of granite.

On Canoe Pond they built a miniature fishing-village, with all its accessories. Besides the dwelling they erected four little wharves, «flakes» (the long tables on which fish are cleaned and split), and fish-houses—all, of course, on a Lilliputian scale. On the pond they had various typical little craft—the dories so characteristic of the New England coast, smacks, lobster-sloops with club-sails, and even a steamer that had clockwork for an engine, and transported fish from the village to a port at the opposite end of Canoe Pond. On a point at the entrance to the village harbor they erected a miniature lighthouse; the shallows in the harbor were buoyed, and on one ledge they set a cage-spindle as a day-mark. The lobster-boats had the regulation lobster-pots, and there were reels for drying the nets, for which latter mosquito-netting was utilized. The boys split and salted minnows at the flakes, packed them in little barrels, and shipped them by steamer to the trading-port across Canoe Pond. Trade was facilitated by money from the Matinicus Rock mint, which issued copper for gold and tin for silver, while cigar-box stamps served as greenbacks. The fame of this fishing-village spread all over Penobscot Bay, fishermen often putting in at Matinicus Rock for a look at it.

Gulls and ducks by the thousands circle about the rock. The gulls make their nests among the broken rocks at the northern end, and the boys found no end of amusement hunting for eggs. They constructed two gunning-stands on the sea-wall, building two sides of loose stones, and roofing them with driftwood, and thus had many a shot at the

A FUNERAL.

end of the rock are filled with a soil so rich that it has been sent for from Matinicus Island, and even from the mainland, for flower-potting. The elder Grant had an old sailor's love of flowers, and he scraped together enough soil from the crevices to make a little patch of ground, and there he planted a flower-garden the beauty of which was noted far and near. The steamers which ply between Boston and St. John, New Brunswick, pass the rock several times a week, but in the night, on their regular trips. Extra trips, however, may bring a steamer of this line to the rock during the day. Of course there is a bond of sympathy between the seafarer and the lighthouse-keeper; and in summer, when it was possible on these extra trips to do so, the captain of the steamer would lay her to abreast of the rock long enough for Captain Grant to put off in a dory with a large bouquet from his garden, and the captain of the steamer would reciprocate with a bundle of newspapers.

ducks as they swam in to feed on the mussels that had been washed up on the ledges. Often the ducks were so numerous that the sportsmen desisted, because gunning would simply have been slaughter.

The little family was not without its sorrow. A sister who had been born on the rock died there, and was buried in a fissure of the granite, the open end of which was walled up with brick. This little soul had never been off the rock. The thirty-two acres of granite about which the sea was ever beating formed her world, and there she now lies at rest.

Some of the crevices near the southern

When I was on Matinicus Rock it had eight inhabitants: the keeper, who is a bachelor; his housekeeper; and the three assistant keepers, one of whom had a family of three girls living on the rock. It was the eldest of these that we met in the dory half-way across from Ragged Island, on her return from school. The second girl had charge of the chickens, but she had not yet been obliged to imperil her life in rescuing them, as Abby Burgess once did. The coop stands picturesquely among the rocks on the southwestern end, a stony path winding in and out among the boulders descending to it. The wind howls about the coop, and the chickens, as they wander over the rocks, can see the spray dashing over the ledges. These chickens are a thoughtful-looking lot. Though well fed, they seem moved to melancholy by the constant surging of the sea about their little world. Even the rooster, who need fear no rival from a neighboring barn-yard, does not strut about with the pride of a bespurred cavalier, and his crowing is saddened by a pathetic overtone.

The ducks—there is a flock of tame ones on the rock—are more in their element. But in winter they, like the chickens, are often storm-bound in their coop several days at a time; and as conversation under such circumstances is apt to flag, they, no doubt, fall to meditating, which probably accounts for their serious air and their disinclination to quack except at infrequent intervals. Perhaps while out of the coop in fair weather they are making mental notes for debate during the next blizzard. The surroundings of their coop are such as to cause even a very dull duck to reflect. It stands with its back to an old boat-house, and is fenced in with lobster-pots and half of an old wherry.

It is said that in desolate stations like that on the rock keepers will sometimes pass days without exchanging a word, not because of any ill will between them, but because they are talked out. I am sure, however, that this never happens on Matinicus Rock. The keeper is one of those kindly souls who always have a pleasant word, and his assistants have caught his spirit. He is a well-read man. Like many of the more intelligent keepers in the service, he manages to make time that would otherwise hang heavy on his hands pass pleasantly by utilizing the little library which the Lighthouse Board supplies, the library being changed from time to time. He has been for some years a subscriber to THE CENTURY, having been first attracted to it by the Lincoln biography and the Siberian articles; and about the time it is due he endeavors, no matter what the weather, to pull across to Matinicus Island for the mail. He performs his duties in a cheerful spirit, and he loves Matinicus Rock. Before coming there he sailed with his father. During the war the Confederate cruiser *Tallahassee* approached the rock. The Grants thought she would shell the towers, but they remained at their posts. They saw her destroy a number of small fishing-vessels, and this so incensed the younger Grant that he forthwith transferred his services to the United States navy. After the war he sailed on the lakes, but he

FLOWERS FOR THE STEAMBOAT.

ENGRAVED BY R. C. COLLINS.

WATCHING THE «TALLAHASSEE» DESTROYING FISHING-BOATS.

missed the smell of salt, and returned to the rock. Like every intelligent seafarer, he appreciates the grandeur of the ocean. «Sometimes after a storm,» he told me, «when I watch the waves bursting over the ledges, I just have to shout to express my feelings.» Another time he said: «I should think the sea would get worn out beating against this old rock.» We were then standing at the northeastern end of the rock, and looking along its high face, with its deep rents and jagged points, and its rough black ledges thrown out like a vanguard to meet the first onslaught of the sea. As the great waves rushed in they burst over these ledges, and sent their spray, now in one huge white mass that, falling back into the fissures, was shattered into myriads of glistening particles, to be blown in nebulous showers before the wind, now whipped into fantastic shapes, now taking the ledges at a leap and landing high upon the rock. Over all blew a fine spray that half veiled the gray towers at the extreme end of the vista. Not far behind us

was the huge boulder which the sea had moved from its original point of rest. We could not see it as we looked at the ocean; but we felt its nearness, so that coupled with the grand scene before us was the sense of the vast power vested in the ocean when it vents its wrath.

The keeper owns the only quadruped on the rock—a cow. This valuable beast is named Daisy. Like the chickens and ducks, Daisy is sensibly affected by her environment. The very method of her landing upon the rocks was enough to cause her to lose faith in human nature during the rest of her existence. She was brought over from Matinicus Island in a small boat, and when within a short distance of the rock the boat was tipped over so far to one side that Daisy lost her balance and fell into the water, where she was left to swim ashore. Although she is an object of affectionate regard to the little community on Matinicus Rock, she does not seem to have forgotten her involuntary plunge. Often I have seen her standing upon that mass of barren granite, the only living thing in view, the wind furrowing up her hide. She would gaze out upon the wild waste of waters with a driven, lonely look, the pathos of which was almost human. The patches of soil on the rock yield about grass enough to last her during the summer. In winter the sear aspect of these patches adds to the desolate appearance of this treeless, shrubless ocean home. Often the cow looks across the reach in the direction of Matinicus Island, and moos pathetically, as if longing to wander over the distant pastures. She formerly found some companionship in a rabbit, with which she was accustomed to play at dusk; but the rabbit died. The cow's existence was again brightened by the birth of a calf. It became necessary, however, to kill the little cow baby, and the mother's grief over the taking off of her offspring was so intense that she refused food for three days.

There are usually several dogs on the rock that are trained to retrieve ducks. At present, however, the cow is the only pet. The keeper once captured a young seal which had been washed up among the ledges, and succeeded in taming it to such a degree that it would drag itself along after him, and whinny when it could not follow him. Attached to the boat-house is a bird-cote, where for several seasons a family of martins has made its home.

One Sunday we had what the keeper called «a regular old grayback of a snow-storm.» During the morning the keeper told me that

Captain Grant had usually conducted a short service while keeper of the lights, and had done so again during his visits to the rock. I offered to read aloud from the Bible and lead in singing a few hymns for as many as would care to join. He was delighted with the suggestion, and in the evening every member of the little community was in the keeper's dwelling, and we had some Bible-reading, chiefly from the Psalms, with the Sermon on the Mount as a substitute for a discourse, interspersed with hymns like « Pull for the Shore,» which, because of the nautical surroundings, I judged would most appeal to the congregation on Matinicus Rock. I do not know that anything has touched me more than the simple earnestness of these worshipers as they lifted their voices above the roaring of the wind and the detonation of the breakers. Life on Matinicus Rock may have its hours of loneliness, but it does not deaden the finer emotions. The ever-surging, ever-sounding sea allows no dweller upon its shores to become a dullard.

The spirit which pervades the personnel of our lighthouse service is well illustrated by an experience of Keeper Grant. The wherry which now forms part of the duck-coop was not always put to such base use. It has known the touch of the sea. Keeper Grant, while an assistant to his father, started in it from the rock one stormy winter day to row over to Matinicus Island. Out in the reach the storm increased, and finally a sea filled the wherry. Its occupant's only safety lay in

ENGRAVED BY A. NEGRI.

AN UNCOMFORTABLE POSITION.

FREDERICK T. HATCH, THE ONLY RECIPIENT
OF THE GOLD BAR FOR HEROISM.

ver medal for rescuing two men from drowning while he was keeper at White Head: and Keeper Marcus A. Hanna, of the Cape Elizabeth light-station, Maine, received the gold medal for the daring rescue of two sailors from a wreck during a severe winter storm.

When the recipient of the gold medal again distinguishes himself by an act of heroism, he is awarded a gold bar, the highest honor the government can bestow. It has been awarded only once, and to a lighthouse-keeper, Frederick T. Hatch, keeper of the Cleveland Breakwater light-station, Cleveland, Ohio. The medal Mr. Hatch received for services performed while a member of the life-saving crew at Cleveland, which rescued twenty-nine persons from two vessels on two successive days during a terrific gale. The gold bar was awarded in February, 1891. A wreck occurred just outside the breakwater at night during a heavy gale and sea. The eight people aboard the wreck, among them the captain's wife, succeeded in reaching the breakwater pier; but the heavy seas swept several of them back, one of them losing his life.

Pulling to the pier in a small boat, Keeper Hatch succeeded in taking off the captain's wife; but she was hardly in the boat before it was swamped and capsized. At the risk of his life, Hatch now seized her. She was utterly exhausted and almost a dead weight; but though nearly overcome himself, he maintained his hold upon her until he could reach a line thrown from the light-station, with which he and his helpless burden were drawn to the lighthouse steps.

Ida Lewis Wilson, whose name is almost as familiar as Grace Darling's, is keeper of the Lime Rock lighthouse in Newport harbor. She received the gold medal for the rescue of two soldiers who had broken through the ice near Lime Rock. In making the award, the government also considered the fact that she had previously rescued at least thirteen persons from drowning.

overturning it and climbing upon the bottom. He had saved an oar, and might easily have made a signal of distress; but he reflected that if his father came off after him, as he would undoubtedly do, and any accident happened to him, only one man, and he elderly, would be left in charge of the lights. Therefore, he simply clung to the bottom of the boat, though he was in peril of being blown out to sea or perishing through exposure in the wintry storm. By a lucky chance the wherry was blown upon Wooden Ball Island, which lies between the rock and Vinal Haven, and he found shelter in the solitary house there.

Keepers in the lighthouse service have, however, done more than display heroism within the duties required of them. A number of them hold life-saving medals from the United States government for feats of heroism performed under the impulse of a higher duty. Keeper Grant's brother, Isaac H. Grant, who married Abby Burgess, holds a sil-

A GRAVE.

Mouth of Cuyahoga River, Cleveland.

FARALLONE ISLANDS AND LIGHT-HOUSE. FROM PAINTING BY JULIAN RIX.

A group of volcanic rocks in the Pacific Ocean about thirty miles west of San Francisco constitute the Farallone Islands. At all seasons of the year they are most forbidding in appearance, and storm-clouds and fog hover over the peaks. There is a light-house on the highest peak of the largest island that is considered one of the most important stations in the world. All ships entering San Francisco have to pass these islands, and they are always dangerous on account of the tides

and waves. The ocean around the islands is never quiet, and the light-house tender that takes supplies out two or three times a year is often compelled to "lay to" for days before a landing can be made. There is only one small cove that answers for a harbor, and in there the waves are always rolling. To make a landing is a difficult matter. The islands are almost devoid of vegetation, but millions of sea-birds make their homes on the barren rocks, and rear their young. The waters on the bar near the islands are the finest fishing-grounds on the coast, and fishing-steamers take out large parties, who generally catch more of the finny tribe than they can carry.

SANKATI LIGHT-HOUSE.

Mouth of the Savannah River.